Magical Parent
Magical Child
The Optimum Learning Relationship

Michael Mendizza
Joseph Chilton Pearce

Special Workshop Edition

Touch the Future
123 Nevada Street, Suite A
Nevada City, CA, 95959
www://ttfuture.org

Contents

Magical Parent–Magical Child
The Optimum Learning Relationship

Foreword by Joseph Chilton Pearce & Michael Mendizza

Part One
The Intelligence of Play

Introduction
Real Jedi Masters Play 3
In the Zone 4
Optimum Learning Relationships 5
Who's Leading Who and Where Are We Going? 11

Intelligence & the Developing Brain
Intelligence—Who, What & Where? 14
Brains Here, Brains There, Brains Everywhere 15
Images, The Brain & Its Operating System 17

Origins of Self As Self-Defense
To Me or Not to Me? That Is the Question 18
Self As Self-Defense 20
Shame and the Origins of Self 21
Becoming As Others See Us 22

Developing Capacity
Stage Specific Learning 24
The Model Imperative 24
Evolution - The Lower Into The Higher 25
Devolution - The Higher Into The Lower 26
Environmental Signals 26

States of Being & Their Meaning
State-Specific Learning 27
Reflexes - Mental, Emotional, Physical Pinball 29
The Magic of Memory 30
The Primacy of States 32
States Are Content 33
Fields of Meaning 34
Sharing Fields 35
The Intelligence of the Heart 36
Insight-Intelligence & Beginner's Mind 39

Play—The Optimum State

The Intelligence of Play 41
Play As Learning 42
Authentic Play—Complete, Selfless Attention & Absorption 43
Four perspectives: Researcher, Scientist, Explorer and the Mystic

Safe Enough to Play

The Safe Place 47
Basic Trust 50
A Lifetime of Experience in a Glance 52
The Learning Channel We Call Bonding 53
Primary Learning & Conditioning 57
Play, Practice & Work 58

Play Ages & Stages

Smiles 61
High Chair Play 62
Toddlers 62
Storytelling 63
Monkey See - Monkey Do 63
Child of the Dream 64
Play-Talk 64
Three's a Crowd 65
Rough and Tumble 66
Groupies 68
No Grown-ups Allowed! 68
Do It Yourself! 69
Television & Computer Play 70
The Art of Play 72
Adult Play 73
Abstract Play 74
Transcendent Play, Sacred Play 75

Rewards & Punishments

Conforming to Expected Patterns 75
It Is All About Control 79
Our Contest Culture 80
Approval of Others 82
What Will They Think of Me? 83
Play Deprivation & Violence 85
Focusing on the Score 86
Whacking, Spanking & Corporal Punishment 86

Athletics & the Intelligence of Play

Adulterating Free Play 89

Intrinsic (Inside) vs. Extrinsic (Outside) Motivation 92

Following the Leader 95

Little League 96

Winning & Losing 97

Magical Parents – Magical Athletes 99

Watching with Wonder 102

The Coach 103

Expanding Our Boundaries 104

Transforming Ourselves—Transforming Culture

Our Brave New Industrial Mind 106

Part Two

Principles for Peak Performance & Optimum Learning

Taking The Lid Off Development, a candid dialogue:
Joseph Chilton Pearce & Michael Mendizza 113

Introduction to Principles 126

Guidelines 128

Becoming Multi-Dimensional Human Beings 128

Principle 1: Being Attentive to Being 129
        (the model imperative)

Principle 2: Safe Enough to Play 131
        (protecting, belonging, the safe place)

Principle 3: Invite the Unexpected 133
        (suspending assumptions)

Principle 4: Take Your Cues From The Child 135
        (the art of listening & observing)

Principle 5: Responding Deeply & Completely 137
        (the awakening of intelligence)

Principle 6: Imagine 139
        (more on television & computers)

Principle 7: Renewing 146
        (reincarnating now)

Playful Parenting—The Optimum Learning Relationship 148

References

Touch the Future Interview Index 153

Recomended Video Programs

Featuring Joseph Chilton Pearce
Reaching Beyond Magical Child, Six One-Hour Programs 154
Mother-Infant Bonding and The Intelligence of the Heart 155

Discovering the Intelligence of Play 156
Golf & The Intelligence of Play 157
The Origins of Love & Violence 158
Babies Know More Than You Think 159

Index 160

Foreword

Our purpose is to transform childhood by transforming adults. We do this by focusing on and optimizing the relationship or interface between children and adults. Helping adults rediscover the "childlike" genius of their own nature, as they guide, learn from and mentor children, awakens and develops in adults new capacities and possibilities. Infusing the adult-child relationship with this innate creative energy and attention transforms the adult and therefore provides a radically different learning environment for child development. Changing the adult changes the environment we call childhood, which transforms the child, which cycles back and transforms the adult. We call this playful, reciprocal-dynamic, the *Optimum Learning Relationship*.

Magical Parent – Magical Child, the Optimum Learning Relationship develops this theme by exploring and applying the psychology of optimum experience to parenting, to childcare, education and to volunteer coaching.

We believe the "state" athletes call the *Zone*, what researchers and professionals refer to as *Flow* and what children call *Play* share the basic characteristic of self-less absorption and complete engagement in the moment. We believe this "state" of complete *unconflicted* behavior is nature's baseline, her expectation, for optimum learning, performance and well-being.

Learning, performance and wellness are "state specific." States are primary; they come first, filter and define what we actually learn, how we perform and our relative wellness or *dis*ease, moment to moment. The actual state of the relationship is the primary "content" of our experience which is learned and remembered, often lifelong, especially for children, regardless of adult intentions.

When adults give attention to "state as content" the playful, dynamic and reciprocal nature of the adult-child relationship becomes the Optimum Learning Relationship for both children and adults. The adult-child relationship becomes a profound opportunity for self-actualization and mastery, a transformative practice every bit as demanding and powerful as found in any monetary, martial art or athletic training camp.

Being natural, a state of ease, grace and tremendous creative force, what then prevents this optimum state from being our norm rather than the exception? Early in a child's life disapproval by adults, "no! don't touch that, do this not that," demands a defensive response. Repeated over and over again with great force and shame, this reaction begins to form as an image, a image of self-as-self-defense. Quickly this defensive self-image habituates and becomes "real" to the child. And with that image and the defensiveness it implies, the essential quality of optimum experience, complete self-less absorption and engagement in the moment, is lost, for many, forever.

Being in the state of play, flow or in the zone present to the child a very different model-environment than authority and threat, punishment and rewards. Not needing to defend themselves the child is free to give total selfless attention and energy to perceive, engage and learn form the moment, deeply and completely. The resources that traditionally go into self-as-self-defense are transformed into optimum learning, performance and wellness, as nature intended by our design.

We view the adult-child relationship as the most fundamental and therefore the most important relationship. What takes place in that adult-child interface, often before a child learns to speak, determines their personal future and the future of humanity.

We all know that childhood is a developmental process for children. Our purpose is to awaken a deep realization that guiding, learning from and mentoring children is a developmental process for adults. When approached in this way the relationship, with its learning and personal development, becomes dynamic, reciprocal and playful. Conflict is reduced transforming all of childhood and adulthood. The results we believe are radically different human beings, and therefore culture, than we see today.

This change can only come about in the interface, the space and learning which occurs between children and adults. By focusing on the inner nature of adults, in relationship with children, adult perceptions and behaviors including the society they create are transformed naturally without resistance. Any attempt to bring about this change in children or in society, without this corresponding deep inner transformation in adults, will inventively lead to conflict and violence.

Part One of the Magical Parent – Magical Child explores this new paradigm. Part Two offers seven principles for cultivating and maintaining Optimum Learning Relationships, at any age, in any field. Complementing and expanding the narrative are selected quotes from Joe's major publications including *Crack in the Cosmic Egg, The Magical Child, Bond of Power,*

Evolution's End and *The Biology of Transcendence*. Our intent is to reveal how the essential concepts which make-up this new model have been woven throughout these previous works. For those familiar with Pearce's collected works, this new volume encapsulates his unfolding inspiration and insights. For those who are just discovering Joe, our hope that the highlights offered here will draw new readers to his past publications. For no one in my view has stretched so far or stitched so many different pieces together in the tapestry of human development..

Michael Mendizza

Research has expanded our knowledge of child development far beyond the boundaries of 25 years ago, when Magical Child was first published. In this little volume we have both updated Magical Child and made a simple summary of those issues bearing on the well-being of child *and parent*.

Research shows that child and parent are like mirrors for each other - each affects the well-being of the other. The parent's state of mind and emotional relations with the child are far more important than standard of living or name-brand clothes. A secure, nurtured child, protected from the interferences of a violent or hostile world-out-there, will grow to be an intelligent, happy adult, able to handle that world, and make parents happy along the way.

Some parents think, "It's a jungle out there. We need to raise a tough child to succeed and survive in that jungle-world." New brain research shows why this notion has not worked well for anyone, child, adult, or society. The best survival in a jungle is to be intelligent, balanced, self-reliant, resourceful, and happy. Then one finds not a jungle but a playground, wherever one is.

Play is the child's royal road to intelligence, creative thinking, and joy. The child who can play will play skillfully and successfully throughout life. People complain that "all children want to do is play." Nature designed children that way. And nature intends, as children mature into adults, to retain their childlike qualities of wonder and lifelong joy of learning. When child grows and becomes the parent it is pricelessly these childlike qualities that will transform parenting into one of life's most powerful learning experience imaginable.

Nature moves for greater intelligence and play is the key that unlocks and develops that intelligence, at any age, in all its varied forms. Following nature's design for play makes a smarter, happier life for all. To be unable to play is unnatural and eventually leads to violence.

Children obviously need boundaries and feel most comfortable within known limits, provided those limits are fair and not arbitrary. Boundaries let a child know that they are important, that they are watched over and cared for. But boundaries can bind. Little children are driven by nature to interact with the objects and events of their world, and their intelligence depends on exploring and learning about that living world around them. To explore is to taste, touch, smell, feel, talk to, listen to, interact with, their immediate environment. "Keep out of reach of children" runs counter to nature's agenda for intelligence. Television is no substitute for the real world. Television can't be tasted, touched, felt, smelt, and talked with.

Discipline comes from a word meaning joyful follower. A child wants to do the right thing and stay in the good graces of parents and family. Children learn by exploring their living world and following the model set by their parents. A child thrives under approval and praise. Children shrink back and build defenses if criticized and continually corrected. NO! and Don't are crippling words and should be used in emergencies only. Real emergencies! The simple guidelines we offer in part two virtually eliminate the need to say No!, to punish and reward children into compliance.

The brain is designed to do one thing, and that is learn, but children can't learn and defend themselves at the same time. Defending one's self splits attention and energy. To explore and learn about the living world, a child must feel secure, safe, accepted, and loved by that world. The parent is the child's first environment, or world.. The child who is driven to doubt his or her acceptance and love by parents is a child whose development will be handicapped.

True learning is play, and effortless. Learning through fear is conditioning, and breeds violence. The child plays and learns if given a safe-space in which to play and learn. Providing the safe space for a child helps parents rediscover their own safe space. The safe-space is love and mutual acceptance. Being in the safe-space creates a different, healthier chemistry of the body than being defensive and on-guard. The safe-space of love breeds health, feeling unsafe and unwanted breeds illness.

Growing with children is a source of learning for the parent. A five year old told her father that children are born to teach their parents to think in their hearts so everything goes well. Otherwise, she said, they think only in their heads and life is hard. A five year old is quite intuitive. (Intuition is the ability to perceive information not present to the senses. If a parent responds positively to a child's intuition, that faculty tends to grow and expand.)

Growing with a child is a challenge and adventure. Nature did not design us to make war with our children, nor for the child to cause parents grief. Nature designed us to love our children and allow them to love us. Love is the safe-space, in which both parent and child can play and where learning takes place naturally. A parent can't teach love. They can only love and the child's natural state unfolds in response to that love. A parent can't love if he or she was never loved when they were children. But the natural state of a child will teach the parent to love in turn, if the parent is tuned in to that child.

Learning to observe a child, accurately "read" a child's state, we discover what a child is actually like. This is an education for a parent and boon for a child. Parents tend to look at children not to find out what their child's nature is like, who their child is, or what state the child is in, but to see if their child's behavior is proper.

Modifying a child's behavior as a matter of principle is arbitrary, becomes judgmental and restrictive. The child senses they are being judged and goes on the defensive. Part of the child's energy-attention is then focused on the parent's judgments and the child's own defense, part on what is to be explored and learned. This means a split attention-energy, prevents concentration and impairs natural learning.

A parent can't love and critically judge at the same time. Nor can the child learn and be judged at the same time. Love brings natural learning. Judgment brings conditioning. The difference between learning and conditioning is the difference between a magical childhood and an unhappy one. For parent and child. The happy child is the brighter child and smarter adult. The following is a guide in discovering and engaging the Optimum Learning Relationship, that we believe is the birthright of every adult and child. May it be a happy voyage.

Joseph Chilton Pearce

For my teachers
Eric, John-Michael, Bonnie
Joe, David, Ashley and K.

Part One

The Intelligence of Play

Introduction

Real Jedi Masters Play

Athletes, martial artists, musicians, dancers—people whose lives depend on peak performance—describe a magical state where extraordinary performance is easy. They call it the *Zone*. In the Zone their personal best flows naturally, without effort. At times even the miraculous feels normal and natural. Researchers call this state of optimal performance *Flow*. Children call it play.

Elite athletes understand that being in a good state rather than in a bad one can make a critical difference in a championship playoff. For centuries being in the Zone was sought after by ancient performance specialists, Zen archers, Yogis, the Samurai, and others. Long ago in a galaxy far away, the Star Wars myth is filled with images of Jedi masters flowing in the Zone. For some women, pregnancy and birth are Zone experiences. Sexual intimacy can be transcendent.

The Zone is not some far-off, mystical fantasy. It is right here, right now, pulsing in every cell of our bodies. Optimum is easy, the miraculous natural when resistance to learning and peak performance are reduced or eliminated. If being in the Zone is good enough for athletes and Aikido masters, why not for you and me? Why not for our children? Imagine learning, performing and parenting "in the Zone," not just in rare moments, but most of the time. Imagine if the resistance and conflict found in most adult-child relationships were reduced or eliminated. Becoming a Jedi master may be easier than we "think." We are "the Force," so why not use it? Our goal is to apply what is known about this optimum state to the most important relationship of all, the relationship between adults and children, right now, at any age, in any field.

In the Zone, *Optimum Learning Relationships* unfold naturally. Magical parents nurture and mentor magical children while magical children challenge and encourage adults to rediscover their own magical nature. The child challenges the adult to discover undreamed of possibilities, and the adult models similar possibilities for the child. In the Zone, parenting, childhood, and learning become a dance, a playful, expansive exploration of new possibilities, optimum learning, and extraordinary performance.

My work inspires such a variety of responses because it explores some very fundamental issues about the human mind and our development as a species: how our experience of the world and of ourselves forms within the "ocean of neurons" in our heads; why the very nature of our brain/mind leads us to "dominion over" the physical world and then beyond that world's boundaries; why we fail to develop and so feel victimized by the world instead; and what simple steps we can take as individuals to complete our natural development and achieve the potential nature intended.
Evolution's End

3

We begin by using sports as a metaphor. Any experience that transcends our ordinary sense of self will do—walking in the woods, creating sand castles at the beach, dancing, childbirth, watching a sunset, making love. Being in the Zone is not about the activity; it is all about our state of being.

In the Zone

In 1995 Michael Murphy, co-founder of Esalen Institute, and researcher Rhea A.White published *In the Zone, Transcendent Experiences in Sports*. The book combined 6,500 sources and stories, from both professional and amateur athletes, stories that described moments of illumination and ecstasy, out-of-body experiences, altered perceptions, and exceptional feats of strength and endurance spanning almost the entire spectrum of sports and physical adventures.

> Sports have enormous power to sweep us beyond our ordinary sense of self, to evoke capacities that have generally been regarded as mystical…The great seers of the contemplative traditions have explored the inner life more deeply than most of us, and they have opened up spiritual territories that we may or may not enter. But many athletes and adventurers have followed partway, however inadvertently, through the doorways of sport.
>
> Michael Murphy, Rhea A. White
> *In the Zone, Transcendent Experiences in Sports*

There is no formula for being in the Zone. It is not just one experience, nor is it limited to athletics. Being in the Zone is not really an activity; rather, it is a unique quality of relationship. It is not the activity that determines great performance; it's our relationship to the activity that counts. Being in the Zone is simply being in an optimum state.

> Acute well-being, peace, calm, stillness, detachment, freedom, weightlessness, ecstasy, power, control, being in the present, mystery, awe, unity, altered or extrasensory perception, flow, optimum experience, and authentic play…What people have in common is that they're describing a state that is beyond their ordinary functioning. If you unfold what they mean, you find that there are hundreds of different ways in which people go beyond ordinary. Our book, <u>In the Zone,</u> catalogued these different experiences and asked

The human brain-mind is designed for functions radically different from and broader than its current use. An astonishing capacity for creative power is built into our genes, ready to unfold. Our innate capacities of mind are nothing less than miraculous, and we are born with a driving intent to express this capacity...
To allow the full development of intelligence, we must acknowledge and cooperate with this biological plan. In so doing, we will find that most of our current problems with infants and children never materialize. For our problems are largely man-made, caused by ignoring nature's plan. Nature herself worked out all the problems aeons ago.
Magical Child.

the question, "Why do they happen?" "How might they be evoked?" If we look for the patterns of activity that lead to these experiences we can be deliberate and start training for them. These are technologies of transformation and the period I think we are now in.

Personal Interview
Michael Murphy
Co-Founder, Esalen Institute, Author, <u>In the Zone</u>, <u>Future of the Body</u>

Johnny Miller, a world-class athlete, discovered the Optimum Learning Relationship on the golf course.

> The strongest energy in the world is love. And if you love what you are doing, you've got a chance to hook on to a clear channel. You become energized, your brain is alert, your body feels strong, your intuitions are there, you have clear thinking; you can be the most that you can be. In 1970 when I went out to win the Phoenix Open, it was like I was playing by myself. I had zero anxiety. No tension. No stress. I was completely confident. When I was over the ball I felt like I was weightless. I had a feeling that I almost could just float off the ground. It was a feeling of confidence but also a warm feeling inside that I was in control. I could dictate my own energy and paint my own picture out on the course. I was able to address every situation and find a creative answer. The shot would talk to me. I'd say fine.
>
> It was so much fun I couldn't wait to hit the next shot. I was taking every shot to the highest level, playing "E" ticket golf. Most golfers are only in the zone for a round or two in their life. I was in it more often, because I would listen to my heart. I did all my homework, but I'd listen to the child in me. I listened to that inner voice.

Personal Interview
Johnny Miller
PGA Hall of Fame

Bonding is the issue, regardless of age. The parent who can start off with a new infant is lucky because by bonding to that infant they are bonding with the undifferentiated primary process (innate intelligence). Learning to take our cues from the child and make a corresponding response means learning to heed and respond to the primary process in ourselves as well. A child can teach us an incredible amount if we are willing to learn, and because s/he is biologically geared to take his/her cues from us, s/he learns as we do.
Magical Child

Imagine being a parent or educator and relating to children in this optimum state. If it's good enough for a golf ball, isn't it good enough for you and the children you love? Do we, or they, deserve anything less?

Optimum Learning Relationships

Optimum means best possible. Learning implies the discovery and perhaps mastery of new patterns or possibilities. Relationship means

Perfection is utilizing all the modes of mind... Perfection is daring to embrace the universe as our true dimension, daring to steal the fire from the gods, to walk on water or fire unafraid, to heal, to claim plenty in times of dearth, to behold boldly that desire and become what we have need to be.
Crack in the Cosmic Egg

connection, interaction, and interdependence. An Optimum Learning Relationship, therefore, is *the* most effective process for children and adults to transcend their individual limitations; to grow and to learn together. Only through such a relationship can we reduce and eliminate the limitations, conflicts, and aggression we impose on ourselves and our children, generation after generation.

Optimum Learning Relationships open the door to the unknown. In these relationships something unexpected is waiting to be discovered. There is no authority, no fixed rules. The child and the adult are moving targets, growing, learning, changing every day. To respond appropriately in such a dynamic and changing relationship, both must be sensitive observers. What was appropriate yesterday, or even a few moments ago, may be completely inappropriate now, this living moment. To give such complete attention requires discipline, deep respect, care and affection.

The word *discipline* often implies obedience, doing what we are told, following one's own or some outside authority, conforming to a pattern. It usually means coercive or forced action, involving rewards and punishments designed to limit or modify behavior. The root meaning of the word *discipline* is *disciple*, which meant originally to be a joyful follower. True discipline involves no coercion, no external rewards or punishments. The disciple joyfully follows the teacher.

The more developed the perceiver, the greater and more alive his reality. To a wise man, a visionary, an artist, or a saint, a tree is more real than to a fool or dullard... Ordinary seeing is mechanical and dead; vision is seeing that the universe is the material for creation, not the fixed deadness of matter.
Bond of Power

In Optimum Learning Relationships the adult follows the child as a teacher as the child follows and responds to the adult. Each follows the "model" and the modeled behavior is precisely what the other needs to "discover" and "learn" at their unique stage of development. For the child, the model may be physical skills, walking, holding a fork, or roller-skating. For the adult the model may be curiosity, spontaneity, or playfulness. Each is guided into new ways of playfully transcending their current limitations.

To follow a model one must be aware that it exists. In Optimum Learning Relationships the primacy of one's "state of being," in relationship, is valued over the information, content, task or challenge of the moment. This attention given to the ever-changing states in relationship occurs naturally in bonded relationships. We can't really see and respond to others as they are while looking out for our agenda, our self interests. A prerequisite to Optimum Learning Relationships is a bond of care and affection.

Learning means the discovery or mastery of new patterns and possibilities. For something new to blossom, there must be an opening, and an ending or suspension of the old, of the known and its "agenda." Optimum Learning Relationships imply a new relationship with knowledge itself, with information, especially the knowledge and beliefs we hold about parenting and learning. Beliefs are very active. They imply an agenda. This is right and this is wrong. The gravity or active quality of our assumptions often blinds us to what is actually going on, this present moment. We often miss or misunderstand what the child is experiencing, expressing, and needing. We see only our agenda, and whether or not our darlings are meeting our expectations, conforming to our image of who they should or should not be.

Entering an Optimum Learning Relationship demands a shift of emphasis from the adult's agenda, a focus on predetermined results, to the place where the child is now, and responding appropriately to the actual needs being expressed in the relationship this very moment. Obviously, the relationship embodies more than just the child. Optimum Learning Relationships value and meet the needs of both child and adult. The relationship is reciprocal. Each is bringing the best out of the other as they meet ever-new and increasingly complex challenges, together.

The highest expression of human love and creativity is mentoring the next generation. This moment may be the first step for the child and for us may be a post graduate experience. In Optimum Learning Relationships the adult and child experience the same act, but from a totally different points of view. Parenting brings us to a higher level of the same growth process as the child. And with that, we really come into our own. Through this Optimum Learning Relationship we begin to catch a glimpse of what our next stage of development is all about, a step that transcends our current limitations.

One has to be in the moment to rediscover the caterpillar for the first time, again, to actually see and feel "what is." Sharing in the child's wonder and curiosity reopens our wonder and curiosity. The bond of affection with a child's innocent state creates a profound shift in the adult. The shift is seeing the child as he or she actually is rather than looking through an agenda. It has been said we can't enter the

No capacity can unfold without an appropriate model and proper nurturing...

A child could imitate, or construct a model of his universe, around any model, and respond accordingly to his construction.

He does model what he is given, and so does as we do. He is blocked not because of some innate lack, but from an outer lack of modes and nurturing...

We do not model our lives according to theories or abstract functions, but according to live, visible, tangible models. We do not bond to universal processes but to persons. The power of the bond can come into our life only through the powers of the bonded person.

Bond of Power

kingdom unless we become little children. Participating in a child's state of innocence and wonder opens the door to the kingdom once again.

Human development ultimately involves spiritual development and parenting is, or can be, a powerful spiritual process. Adults discovering and opening to their next stage of development, by serving a child they truly love, transforms the meaning of parenting and of education. In taking this step, one discovers that human development, which is our own development, is infinitely open-ended. We, and our children, approach the infinite nature-of-our-nature through stages. Each stage has boundaries. The growth, learning, and development we experience at each stage ultimately means exploring and transcending the boundaries of that stage.Optimum Learning Relationships become a playful spiritual process for those willing to leave behind the limitations they have accepted about themselves and their children.

Environment and genetics are a paired dynamic. As with creator and created they give rise to each other, interdependent to an indeterminable extent. The mother is the sole environment for the first nine to twelve months after birth and the most critical part of the child's environment for the first three to four years.
The Biology of Transcendence

The current approach to parenting, and to education, often means just the opposite. We deny the child's and our own infinite nature by punishing and rewarding children into accepting and conforming to the same limited patterns we have accepted. We validate our limitations by imposing them on our children.

Culture is bound together by certain ways of thinking. How we perceive ourselves and our children is formed by this cultural model. Conforming to the limitations of culture can never transcend the problems culture creates. A completely different approach is needed.

Optimum Learning Relationships provides a way for each individual parent, coach, childcare provider, and educator to create a new set of boundaries for themselves and for the children they love, a wider set that reaches beyond the punitive parental-teacher models we all know so well. Optimum Learning Relationships free parents from the limitations imposed by their own conditioning. In freeing the children they love from accepting false limitations the adult becomes free. Cultural patterns and beliefs, which are implicitly aggressive, are replaced by sensitive, aware, intelligent attention. And this intelligent attention "acts" naturally, spontaneously for the well-being of all.

Optimum Learning Relationships invite adults to discover evolution's next step forward, hand in hand, with each new life. The tools for this new relationship are sensitive awareness, affection, the art of listening and true observation, intuition, playful intelligence, and insight. By taking our cues from the child we discover and create, right now, this moment, the appropriate response. True observation and intuition inevitably lead to new insights, and new insights lead to new models. Playful, always fresh, ever new and challenging, the child is the teacher of the adult and the adult is the teacher of the child. Their relationship becomes the ultimate classroom for both.

The parent-child dance begins anew each moment with simple awareness of the state of their "being" in relationship. Affection surrounds them, protects them in an atmosphere of trust, safety, and mutual respect. They listen and observe with great care and clarity, as if just that moment having discovered some unknown treasure. Each takes their cues from the other, suspending fixed assumptions of how they should or should not be. They connect, not with ideals and expectations, rather "as they are," that moment. The ever-changing dynamic of their "actual relationship" becomes the object of playful exploration and novelty, play being the act of learning and learning being pure play. The limitless realm of imagination reveals new patterns and possibilities. New insights are embodied which transform the relationship. And the cycle repeats, the next moment and the next, playful, always fresh, dynamic, and ever so challenging.

Is such a relationship just another ideal, a fantasy? We don't think so. The dynamic qualities found in Optimum Learning Relationships seem to reflect the underlying principles found in the scientific theory know as Chaos. John Briggs and F. David Peat in *Seven Life Lessons of Chaos* define chaos theory as the study of the underlying interconnectedness that exists in apparently random events. "Chaos science focuses on hidden patterns, nuance, the "sensitivity" of things, and the "rules" for how the unpredictable leads to the new." Percolating through the lessons of chaos are three underlying themes, which, when applied to our lives and relationships, can reduce stress and conflict and enhance creativity: Control, Creativity, and Subtlety.

Life is uncertain, the scientists say. We humans feel this uncertainty more keenly because our consciousness allows us to remember past injuries and project new disasters into the future. The major use of our creative and intellectual capacity, down through the ages, has been to eliminate uncertainty by predicting and controlling nature and

Existence is from the Latin "existere," meaning to be set apart. Without separation there can be no diversity, no creation, no experience, no love, longing, and subsequent union. What we long for in each other is perfect relationship. Out of perfect relationship comes the unity we seek, a unity that exists only within us. Finding that point of unity within, love and compassion for all creation, expressions of our own selves, is boundless.
Evolution's End

9

ourselves. The essence of traditional parenting, enculturation really, and most of what we call education is "being in control" or "predicting and controlling" the behavior of children. The true nature of children—their complexity and open-ended possibilities—places them well beyond our attempts to predict, manipulate and control. Eventually every parent and educator discovers this obvious fact, much to their dismay. Chaos theory suggests that instead of resisting this unpredictable nature, which is our nature and that of our children, we should embrace it, explore it, play, learn and be transformed by it. Optimum Learning Relationships do just that.

The second basic principle of chaos is creativity. True creativity blossoms when there are cracks in our systems of prediction and control. Physicists David Bohm and F. David Peat describe "creative perception" in *Science, Order, and Creativity* as an extremely perceptive state of intense passion and high energy that dissolves the excessively rigidly held assumptions implicit in commonly accepted knowledge. This sounds very close to the quality of attention found in optimum learning relationships. Creative parenting, a component of Optimum Learning Relationships, unfolds when assumptions about what "should or should not be" a good child or a good parent are suspended. This opens the possibility for something truly new to slip though the cracks of our efforts to predict and control the future. Suspending assumptions frees perception to attend to more subtle process.

There remains a certain feyness, a childlike quality, in all great creative people. In them, somehow, a thread remains intact between their modes of thought. It is a return to this primary-process thinking which brings about metanoia, conversion, the Eureka! illumination of creative thinking.
Crack in the Cosmic Egg

> Old-fashioned logic and linear reasoning clearly have their place, but the creativity inherent in chaos suggests that actually living life requires something more. It requires an aesthetic sense—a feeling for what fits, what is in harmony, what will grow and what will die. Making a pact with chaos gives us the possibility of living not as controllers of nature but as creative participators… To sacrifice control and live creatively requires attention to the subtle nuances and irregular orders going on around us…Chaos theory shows us how apparently tiny and insignificant things can end up playing a major role in the way things turn out. By paying attention to subtlety, we open ourselves to creative dimensions that make our lives deeper and more harmonious.
>
> John Briggs, Ph.D. and F. David Peat, Ph.D.
> *Seven Life Lessons of Chaos*

The more we learn through personal experience, the more we *can* learn; the more phenomena and events with which we interact, the greater our ability for more complex interactions. Can you imagine a more complex and dynamic learning experience than the challenge of nurturing and developing the open-ended intelligence of a new human being? Meeting this intelligence as it is—changing, expanding, creating new patterns and possibilities each day, is a tremendous challenge, a profound responsibility, and a great privilege. Our lives are transformed by responding to the actual needs of the children we love. Discovering that our state of being, moment to moment, is their model, and their state is ours, brings about increased awareness and sensitivity to our own behavior. Only love is powerful enough to bring about such a radical change in perception. Awakening to the deep conditioning we find in ourselves, and not wanting to impose our limitations on our children, is powerful catalyst for our own transformation. With abiding affection and basic trust the child leads the adult playfully into their next stage of development while the adult leads the child playfully into their next stage. And this magical state continues, expanding playfully, lifelong. Yes, this is indeed the Optimum Learning Relationship.

Culture is a circular stalemate, a kind of mock tautology, self-generative and near involute. That we are shaped by the culture we create makes it difficult to see that culture is what must be transcended. Which means we must rise above our notions and techniques of survival itself, if we are to survive.
The Biology of Transcendence

Who's Leading Who and Where Are We Going?

Our proposal is very simple. Optimum is nature's base-line for growth. Children normally enter the world in this optimum state at which point adults normally begin the long process of adulterating their childlike qualities in well-meaning attempts to make children as adult-like as possible. Very early children are rewarded and punished out of the zone, leaving adults feeling quite satisfied that they have done a good job as parents, educators and coaches.

In Optimum Learning Relationships childlike qualities, marked most notably by explosive learning, are shared. The adult is transformed by the child as much as the child is transformed by the adult. Ashley Montagu, a friend and author of fifty books, many of which are classics in human development, referred to this *reciprocal dynamic* as "growing young."

> The truth about the human species is that in body, spirit, and conduct we are designed to grow and develop in ways that emphasize

11

rather than minimize child like traits. We are intended to remain in many ways childlike; we were never intended to grow "up" into the kind of adults most of us have become.

The great rule is: Play on the surface, and the work takes place beneath... Growth of intelligence is never a conscious process: conceptual changes always take place below awareness.

Magical Child

What, precisely, are those traits of childhood behavior that are so valuable and that tend to disappear gradually as human being grow older? We have only to watch children to see the clearly displayed: curiosity is one of the most important; imaginativeness; playfulness; open-mindedness; willingness to experiment; flexibility; humor; energy; receptiveness to new ideas; honesty; eagerness to learn; and perhaps the most pervasive and most valuable of all, the need to love. All normal children, unless they have been [adulterated] corrupted by their elders, show these qualities all day every day of their childhood years. They ask questions endlessly; "Why?" "What is it?" "What's it for?" "How does it work?"

They watch, and they listen. They want to know everything about everything. They can keep themselves busy for hours with the simplest toys, endowing sticks and stones and featureless objects with personalities and histories, imagining elaborate stories about them, building sagas that continue day after day, month after month. They play games endlessly, sometimes carefully constructing the rules, sometimes developing the game as they go along. They accept changes without defensiveness. When they try to accomplish something and fail, the are able to do it another way, and another, until they find a way that works. They laugh—babies learn to laugh and smile before they can even babble—and children laugh from sheer exuberance and happiness. Unless they suspect they may be punished for it, they tell the truth: they call the shots as they see them. And they soak up knowledge and information like sponges; they are learning all the time; every moment is filled with learning. How many adults retain these qualities into middle age?...

Most adults stop any conscious effort to learn in their early adulthood, and thereafter never actively pursue knowledge or understanding of the physical world we inhabit in any form. It is as though they believed that they had learned all they needed to know, and understand it all, and had found the best possible attitude toward it, by age eighteen or twenty-two or whenever they stopped their formal schooling. At this time they begin go grow a shell around this pitiful store of knowledge and wisdom; and from then on vigorously resist all attempts to pierce that shell with anything new....

The entire effort of the educating and training of children was [and is] aimed at making adults of them as soon as possible...The closer their behavior to that of adults the better...Imagination was [and is] frowned upon, even feared; curiosity was [and is] derided ("Curiosity killed the cat!"); free playfulness and humor were [and is] discouraged; open-mindedness was [and is] thought to be heretical; and honesty was [and is] often considered simple rudeness. As for the most precious of all childlike qualities, the eagerness to learn; it was accepted by adults only so long as the subject was [and is] a "proper" one; otherwise it was [and is] forbidden....

Children who failed to thrive under this Spartan regime were themselves blamed for their failure [as is often the case today with the use of Ritalin and Prozac]. It occurred only to a few people that perhaps the fault lay in the failure of the adult world to understand the nature of childhood, and in fact to understand the development of human beings...

Adults fail to understand that those childlike qualities constitute the most valuable possession of our species, to be cherished, nurtured and cultivated [all the days of our lives]. They fail to realize that the child surpasses the adult by the wealth of his possibilities. In a very real sense infants and children implicitly know a great deal more concerning may aspects of growing than adults; adults, therefore, have more to learn from them about such matters than the latter have to learn from adults....

Children are mediaries, the go-betweens who, whenever we allow them to, help us discover our way toward humanity; in bringing them up we face ourselves, as in a mirror, in a clearer, brighter light.

Ashley Montagu
Growing Young, The Genius of Childhood, Recaptured

Intelligence is not assigned only to the brain and nervous system. Every cell of our bodies is an intelligence of staggering complexity, and every cell acts intelligently. The mind-brain is a wonderful array of intelligences ranging from the simpler life forms of the cell and old brain to the most complex. Each human being contains the pattern of all thinking forms developed over the millennia.
Magical Child

Intelligence & The Developing Brain

Intelligence—What Is It & Where?

The oldest evolutionary brain in our head, you recall, the reptilian or hindbrain, provides for fast reflexes; is geared to brute strength driven by primary survival instincts hard-wired for defense; is reflexive, not reflective, and not very negotiable. The forebrain, on the other hand, gives rise to our intellectual, verbal and creative mind, slower, reflective, and far more intelligent and negotiable than that defensive, hair-triggered and reflexive hindbrain.

The Biology of Transcendence

The advice of the King given to Alice in Wonderland was "to begin at the beginning, continue to the end, and then stop." Good advice indeed. We begin our exploration of Optimum Learning Relationships by questioning, "What is intelligence, and where do we find it?"

Ultimately, intelligence can't be defined, for any definition is limited and intelligence is not. We can say that intelligence expresses in living systems as a movement toward wholeness, for coherence and well-being, of the organism and its environment, for the two are not separate. Most of us think of intelligence as brains, mission control, grand central station. Yes, there is a lot of activity going on upstairs, more than we can possibly imagine. The closer we look, however, the more we find that intelligence is spread throughout the entire body and all of nature.

If we look for intelligence only in the brain, we see a very limited picture, indeed. At least 60 percent of the cells that make up the human heart are neurons, like the cells found in the brain. All the basic functions needed for the human body to thrive—movement, nutrition, elimination, reproduction, awareness, and yes, even intelligence—are found in every living cell. Life is holographic. Each part contains a pattern of the whole. Intelligence is everywhere and we are that intelligence. We *are* in touch with and touched by light, sound, heat, odors, tastes, emotions, ideas, thoughts, beliefs, traditions, and much more every moment.

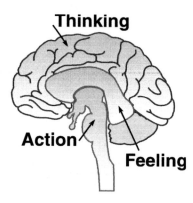

Thinking

Action

Feeling

The pattern of relationships that makes each of us unique includes galaxies of contacts and connections found inside the boundary of our skin and a universe of forces outside. What we call "me" is this galaxy of relationships, incredibly small and incredibly vast, fading off to infinity in all directions.

Brains Here, Brains There, Brains Everywhere

Some relationships help us grow, others hold us back. To appreciate Optimum Learning Relationships we must understand what it means to be related. Relationship means contacts, connections, and interdependence. Nature has developed complex systems to monitor, interpret, and act upon these close encounters. Yes, we call these systems "brains." As we explore some basic theories about the brain, keep in mind that the brain itself is not intelligence, nor does it create or possess intelligence, any more than a computer is intelligent. Intelligence is much vaster, much more subtle than any of the forms that intelligence creates.

The human brain and nervous system are made of different parts, and each part contributes to the ever-changing relationship we call living. The brain is unique. Among other things, it has the miraculous ability to take a slice of *all* the variable forms and energies that make up the world "out there" and build a *resonant representation* or an *internal image* of that slice. And then, within its limitations, the organism can act upon these images.

> Over 600 million years ago, with the appearance of the cold-blooded vertebrates, there appeared sensory systems, which could construct a resonant representation, or images, of some portion of the external world. The life of cold-blooded vertebrates, what I call one-brain creatures, is limited to the spectrum of sensors and imaging capacity of this basic core brain. The primary function of this core or reptilian brain is survival; food, reproduction and defense.

> About 200 million years ago, elements of what Paul MacLean refers to as the limbic brain, or the second brain, began to appear. The core brain senses and represents an image of the external world. The second or limbic brain monitors and images bodily states—the complex inner world of dynamic metabolism and motions, what we call emotions.

Without exception, these cultural techniques or tools involve carefully masked threats. These threats concern our rapidly learned fear of pain, harm, or deprivation, and our more primal anxiety over separating or alienation from parent, caretaker and society. No matter how we camouflage our intent, to our selves and to our child, all parenting and education (except Waldorf and the best of Montessori) is based on: "Do this or you will suffer the consequences." This threat underlies every facet of our life from our first potty training through university exams, doctoral candidates' orals, employment papers, income tax, on and on infinitum down to official death. Culture is a massive exercise in restraint, inhibiting, and curtailment of joy, on behalf of pseudo and grim necessities.
We live our lives in the long shadow cast thereby.
The Biology of Transcendence

15

As we move up the evolutionary ladder we see increasingly dense neural structures and with them the emergence of curiosity, not for food, not for survival, but curiosity for its own sake. Later still emerged the capacity to create various types of abstract images - of letters, words, numbers, of comparisons, analogies and similarities. This third brain imaged logical sequences and played with symbols, words, colors, sounds, and forms. Imagination was born.

Lizards live in a one-dimensional world. They have fixed habit patterns that react and respond only to the present. They have very poor memories. Two-brain creatures develop an enormous ability to store and recall, remember past experiences. But the second brain has little capacity to reach into the future. With the appearance of the third brain there is a sudden extension into the future, built upon the second brain's past and the first brain's present. With that extension life takes on a three-dimensional perspective. Now we get a three-dimensional perspective which gives rise to the inner representation, or the subjective experience, of an independent "I."

Personal Interview
Keith Buzzell, M.D.

Our worldview is a cultural pattern that shapes our mind from birth. It happens to us as fate. We speak of a child becoming "reality-adjusted" as he or she responds and becomes a cooperating strand in the social web. We are shaped by this web; it determines the way we think, the way we see, what we see. It is our pattern of representation and our response sustains the pattern. Yet any world view is arbitrary to an indeterminable extent. The arbitrariness is difficult to recognize since our world to view is determined by our worldview.
Crack in the Cosmic Egg

Our oldest brain centers monitor and create images (or resonant representations) of different external energy patterns: all the things we touch, see, smell, hear, and taste outside. Other sensors inside the body monitor how we relate to or feel about these close encounters, which include the immune system, the maintenance of hormonal balances, and myriad of other systems and processes. As we move throughout the day external and internal sensors are constantly updating the information gathered from billions of new contacts. This ever-changing flow of information is represented in the body-mind as images or feelings: good, bad, happy, sad, and so on. In his compelling neurobiological account of consciousness and the self, *The Feeling of What Happens,* Antonio Damasio, one of the world's most respected neuroscientists, describes this vast complexity of contacts and connections occurring each moment. We are these contacts and connections, known or unknown, always new, always changing. We are like a river, flowing.

The word (connections) refers to the connection of things and events as it may have occurred historically; it refers to the mental imagetic representations of these things and events as we experience them; and it also refers to the neural connection among brain circuits necessary to hold the record of things and events and redeploy such records in explicit neural patterns…

Antonio Damasio, M.D., Ph.D.
The Feeling of What Happens

The multitasking Windows we find in our computers is no match for the brain in terms of its capacity to simultaneously display physical, emotional, and symbolic images. While sleeping, past, present, and perhaps even future images may be displayed as dreams. Perception, awareness, what we call reality is an ever-changing blend of multiple data streams—external, internal, past, imagined, and intuitive—simultaneously displayed in consciousness. It took nature billions of years to develop this amazing capacity and we take it for granted, which is part of the miracle.

Images, The Brain & Its Operating System

It is perfectly natural for the brain to translate experience into images. That is what the brain does; it communicates information through images. Instant replays of memories are displayed as images, complete with the physical and emotional qualities of the original experience. Present sensations may trigger memories of past experiences, which are displayed as images. One memory can cause another memory to explode into awareness. Archetypes, those ancient patterns buried deep in the structure of our cells, may mix in and out of our daily reality. Images can emerge from intuition, telepathy, or direct insight. Dreams are experienced as images.

Reality is an ever-changing flow of images. Some images are more powerful than others. Of the billions of contacts we experience each day, only a few are intense or meaningful enough to warrant our awareness. A physical sensation, hitting our thumb with a hammer, for example, may, for a moment, occupy all of our attention. We may be overwhelmed by joy or grief and not notice a mosquito nibbling our ear. A story may carry us into an enchanted world of imagination, leaving the "real" world far from view. Past, present, and imagined images all contribute to the moving mental mix we call "me."

An individual undergoes disordering it seems, according to his or her culture's disorder.... we have no choice but to identify with the constructions we make, which we must make. Since we must pattern ourselves and our worldview after our culture and parents, when that is a disordered system for modeling, we are ourselves disordered in precisely the same way. To say that our disorder must be reordered, then, is to say that our conceptual structure, which our whole nature must strive to maintain... must be reconstructed. The initial warp in our developmental drive for wholeness and autonomy must, by the very nature of our brain's drive for that development, be interpreted by us as a threat to autonomy and will be resisted at all costs... Our disorder can't help but drive continuously to maintain its disorder... The force which alone can straighten us out is insight-intelligence operating through consciousness.
Bond of Power

The Origins of Self As Self-Defense

To Me or Not to Me? That Is the Question

Life is relationship. What we experience (the universe) and how we feel about our experience (who we are) creates a portrait or reflection of an ever-changing pattern of relationships. We do not normally think of ourselves as ever-changing patterns of relationships. We think of ourselves as *me*—Joe, Heather, Michael, or Mary. We have accepted the very strange idea that we have a permanent identity, a self-image. Joe is Joe whether he is dressed in yellow or blue. Mary may look and behave differently at different ages, but Mary is Mary. Or so it seems. Michael is always here, eyes open or shut, awake or dreaming. We take our self-image for granted. It feels so normal and necessary. But where does Heather begin and end? Is she ever really the same? Is the image she has about herself accurate? If Heather's self-image is just an image, why does she feel hurt if someone makes an unflattering remark? Do images have feelings? Can images be hurt? It may be that the images we perceive as ourselves are not at all what they appear to be.

Antonio Damasio, again in *The Feeling of What Happens,* describes two selves. One he calls the core self; the other he calls the autobiographical self. The core self is the body-brain linkages, neural and hormonal, and all the systems and circuits which allow the body to perform, more or less reliably, for a lifetime. We might call it our physical self. We experience this core or physical self through an immediate feedback process called *proprioception.* Close your eyes and move your arm around behind your back. Moment by moment, even as the movement is taking place, you know where your hand is in relationship to the rest of the body. The same is true for feet, legs, head, the entire body. Proprioception, this immediate sensing of the physical body, its nature and genetic history, gives rise to the experience of our core self. Damasio states: "[V]irtually all of the machinery behind core consciousness and the generation of core self is under strong gene control." In other words, the experience of a core self emanates directly from our biological history. Aspects of this core self are clearly transgenerational. We inherit hair and eye color from our parents. Sensitive responses to stress we call allergies are often

Perception (what we are aware of as that tasted, touched, felt, smelled or heard) is the end result of a vastly complex and mysterious process. And process always means procedure, movement, action, never a specific "thing." As this is true for our perceptions of the concrete world out there, so it is true of our perception of our own thought process, knowledge and abilities.
Magical Child

Socialization is positive and based on pleasure. Enculturation is negative, and based on pain and fear. Socialization opens us to our higher intelligences and creative play. Enculturation plays on our instincts for defense.
The Biology of Transcendence

inherited. Expressing through this core self are remnants of past generations trailing back to the origins of life itself. All of these "past lives" and the "fields of meaning" they emit are expressing themselves as our core self right now. By this definition, all living systems, regardless of size or complexity, experience some form of core self, unique to their species.

The development of the autobiographical or psychological self is a different matter. As living systems grew more complex, they evolved increasing capacities for memory—physical, emotional, symbolic, and perhaps memories or expressions of nonmaterial fields, a subject we will explore in more detail later. As with the core self, the structures that support the development of autobiographical memory mature and are dependent on inherited biology. The experiences that create the specific content of autobiographical memory—experiences unique to each individual—are dependent on and regulated by the environment: family, home, social influences, culture. And it happens so naturally. We encounter an intense experience, either pleasurable or painful and an image of this experience is recorded as memory. This is repeated over and over again, building up patterns of personal images, day after day. Most often, when we refer to our "self" we are describing the images associated with our environmental history.

Clearly what we call our self is not a fixed or permanent entity. Rather, our self-image is made of many images, some very old, some inherited from our parents, others the result of experiences before birth, some from childhood. Other images emanate from more recent events, perhaps something that occurred yesterday or even this morning. What we call our self is made of all these influences, any one of which may, at any given moment, be screaming loudly, or silently lying dormant.

Why do we identify with these images? Why do we justify and defend these images as though they were an independent or permanent entity? What role does self-image play in optimum experience? In what way does it contribute or hinder? The evidence suggests that Optimum Learning Relationships begin when justifying and defending the image ends. It is really that simple. The less energy we invest in justifying and defending our self-image, the more attention and intelligence we have for learning and performance. Learning and performance increase as the demands imposed by our self-image decrease.

That a mother in the safe place produces a strikingly different brain and child physiology than one in an anxiety space clearly illustrates and expands on nature's Model Imperative. The mother is the model of the eventual child on every level, and a new life must shape according to the models life itself affords. For, as is true in all cases of nature's Model Imperative, the character, nature, and quality of the model determine, to an indeterminable extent, the character, nature and quality of the new intelligence that manifests.
The Biology of Transendence

The images we have of ourselves feel very important, perhaps supremely important, and extend beyond our physical and environmental histories to encompasses everything we have learned, all our beliefs, likes, dislikes, and opinions. If someone challenges a strong belief it feels like they are attacking "me." We take it personally. Are beliefs part of our self-image? Apparently they are. Just about everything we know becomes part of the image, and we construct from these images an individual identity. Historically, the idea that all of us are unique "individuals" is quite new.

> Identity [in the Middle Ages] was not personal but communal, a matter of affiliation, status, and role. One was a Baker or a Smith, perhaps a Goldsmith, or one was Matt's son; that was all the ID that was needed either for external recognition or internal self-assurance... The term "individual" in its medieval usage meant only "one of a class" (as we might speak of an individual pearl or paramecium); not until the latter part of the sixteenth century, when feudal institutions and obligations were largely dissolved throughout Europe, when status had given way to contract and the entrepreneur was buying out the lord of the manor, did the modern sense of the individual "qua" individual—a man for himself—come into currency.
>
> Ashley Montagu
> *The Dehumanization of Man*

It is worth considering that our self-image is really not a thing. It is a response, a process, more like a stream, than something fixed or permanent. The image comes into being only when it is active, when energy is moving. What triggers this energy is a threat, any threat, real or imagined.

Self As Self-Defense

Why do our palms sweat when we step up to the first tee or meet someone for a first date? Why do we get nervous just before we make a public speech? Because we feel threatened. We feel some need to defend ourselves. What will they think of me if I do something stupid? The image rises to the surface most often when we feel threatened. Research reveals a peculiar absence of self-image (and its defense) during moments of extraordinary learning and performance. When we feel safe, completely safe, and engaged in the present mo-

Enculturation is a remedy prescribed by culture for the disease of culture itself and we are impelled to administer this prescription to our young out of our genuine concern for them as well as for ourself. How many times do we hear parents, reflecting on their child's future, ruefully point out, "Man! It's a jungle out there!" The jungle is culture, the predators enculturated humans. Culturally engendered prescriptions for child rearing mask culture as the cause of our pain and breed a new generation locked into culture as the only remedy of itself. This remedy propels us into a lifetime spent correcting culture's supposed failings, to make it less painful, never noting that each correction of culture strengthens that culture and produces more of its painful restrictions.
The Biology of Transcendence

ment or activity, our self-image disappears.

> Real learning happens without a formula in your head. When Joe Montana used to drop back to pass, he wasn't thinking, "Okay, he's running out to the right and I've done this play before." No, he's completely enmeshed in the action. Time disappears. When that happens, you disappear. You literally disappear. What exists is the game and the play and the joy. Joy happens when you disappear. It's not about you. It's about the play and the people.
>
> Personal Interview
Fred Shoemaker
Performance Specialist, Extraordinary Golf

Shame and the Origins of Self

We described how the images that make up what we experience as "self" emanate from our personal history. According to Allan Schore, Ph.D., author of the ground-breaking book *Affect Regulation and the Origin of Self: The Neurobiology of Emotional Development,* our self-image begins to form between twelve and eighteen months of age, when we leave the safety of mother's arms and become mobile. Increased mobility brings with it greater risk. To temper our wild explorations mom, dad and caregivers begin to say "No." Every nine minutes a No! or Don't! blocks the toddler at the time of his or her life when the greatest learning is designed to take place. "No" is a threat and threats must be defended against. The defensive response to a perceived threat creates the image.

Schore states: "The mother utilizes facially expressed stress-inducing shame transactions which engender a psychobiological missatunement with the mother." The mother accuses the child just by her look. Her accusative look warns the child that the action he or she is taking or is about to undertake will break the bond. This becomes a permanent imprint and we carry that accusing face with us, lifelong.

Driven by nature's imperative to explore the world, the child is now threatened if he or she does so by the caregiver—with whom he or she is equally driven to maintain the bond. The resulting conflict sets up the first major wedge in the infant's mind. The toddler and young child will maintain what integrity they can, but eventually will split and become one of us. We then speak of the emergence of the child's "social self," by which we mean he or she has adopted the

Everything is only preparatory for something else that is in formation, as day must fade into night and night into day...
The progression of matrix shifts from concreteness towards abstraction, or from the purely physical world of the womb, mother, earth, and body, to the purely mental world of thought itself. The cycle unfolds according to a genetic timetable that is roughly the same in all cultures.
Magical Child

enculturated mask we adults have learned to wear. And this is the mask we and they eventually identify with, become, and defend, forgetting who we really are.

Over time our reaction to "No, don't touch that," "Do this, not that," becomes a pattern, a conditioned reflex. Whenever we feel threatened, physically or psychologically, there is a loss of safety, a loss of love that demands a defense. The defense is the image which, very early in life, feels normal, real and permanent. Reduce or eliminate the threat and the need for the defensive image disappears. When the image disappears, the energy and attention used to sustain the image can be playfully invested in learning and performance: pretty simple.

Becoming As Others See Us

Young children don't discriminate between their authentic nature and their behavior. They *are* their behavior. For the early child, winning approval and dodging disapproval can be a matter of survival. Survival means fitting into the existing social structure. Self-worth, and by implication self-image, is defined by how well we do this. Ashley Montagu points out that "We not only see ourselves as others see us, we *become* ourselves as others see us."

Just how sensitive are we to external signals? Recent discoveries in genetics confirm that environmental signals cause genes to express and even mutate new forms in relationship to the changing environment. In a thirty-year study of environmental influences on the brain, published under the title *Enriching Heredity*, Marian Diamond, Ph.D., at the University of California Berkeley, demonstrated measurable changes in the brain, at any age, in response to internal and external changes in the environment. In just four days her laboratory mice grew new brain structures in response to environmental signals. If the physical structures of brains adapt so quickly to environmental signals, imagine how these signals impact more subtle processes such as thoughts, feelings, and self-image.

Jean Leidloff, author of the *Continuum Concept*, having lived in the Amazon jungle for four years with Stone Age Indians, put it this way:

> The negative experiences we had in infancy and childhood—are
> no less traumatic than the positive experiences we expected to or

Jean Piaget spoke of a major characteristic of childhood being "an unquestioned acceptance of the given." To the early child everything is as it is, wonderful, exciting, inviting and entrancing, drawing, pulling one into total and complete rapport, involvement and interaction with the world. The child accepts the world as it is since the world is his or her material for imaginative transformation. Once shame is imprinted there will never again be "unquestioned acceptance of the given," but a faltering hesitancy as doubt intrudes and clouds that child's knowledge of self and world.
The Biology of Transcendence

should have had and didn't. The residue of those bad experiences and missed good experiences takes the form of beliefs we have about ourselves; that we can never do anything right, or we're not lovable. Or we have to take care of everyone.

These beliefs are instilled in us in infancy, before we're able to judge anything. We cannot look in the mirror and say; "well I'm a nice little girl. I've got all my fingers and toes and I'm a sweet little thing. I'm intelligent and charming and I got a little pink party dress and I'm just fine." We can't do that. We get our feeling of worth about ourselves and everything else from our authority figures. This is what children do. They take the authority of these people and believe it. Whatever it is. This becomes the basic feeling we have about self and also about the relationship between self and other. We don't need to empower children to trust their nature. The tendency to trust is there. We simply need to allow them to do so.

We should never do anything to a child that will make him feel badly about himself. But we do this all the time. We do it with words and we do it with looks. We only know two ways to treat our children. One is the punishing/blaming: "you are very bad, go stand in the corner or I'll spank you." The other is permissive: "that's perfectly all right darling, if you want to walk on mothers face, she doesn't mind." We don't know any other way.

There is another way. It is called information. If you thoroughly understand that children are innately social, then you understand that what they want is information. You don't have to be angry to tell them what's needed. You just let them know. The idea is not to blame, and not to praise, because both are insulting. Expect children to do the right thing. You then are being a clear model and there's no conflict. It's the way nature designed us to behave.

Personal Interview
Jean Leidloff
Author of <u>The Continuum Concept</u>

The mind-brain is designed for astonishing capacities, but its development is based on the infant and child's construction of knowledge of the world as it actually is. Children are unable to construct this foundation because we unknowingly inflict on them an anxiety-conditioned view of the world (as was unknowingly inflicted on us.) Childhood is a battleground between the biological plan's intent, which drives the child from within, and our anxious intentions, pressing the child from without.
Magical Child

Developing Capacity

Stage Specific Learning

Researchers recognize that there are "stages," or optimum periods for development of different skills and capacities. Life is a treasure hunt. We begin as little children uncovering and developing the physical, emotional, and mental treasures woven into our nature, and this development unfolds in stages. The earliest stages—pregnancy, birth, and the first three years—are the most important. The neural networks for all later stages are created during these early years. Everything that follows is built on this foundation.

Developmental stages unfold in rough blocks. The three trimesters of pregnancy are followed by stages at one, two, four, seven, eleven, fifteen and eighteen years. Early stages focus primarily on physical, sensory motor development. Emotional capacities unfold next. Critical and creative thinking skills follow. The newest region of the brain, the forebrain or prefrontal lobes that may hold the key to transpersonal or spiritual development, matures in the early twenties. Rich and complete development of one stage provides a strong foundation for the next. Compromised development at any stage limits those that follow.

A higher system can incorporate a lower one into its service and transform the lower. Or the converse can happen. The higher can be incorporated into the service of the lower and the transformation is reversed, inverted. In our legends and fairy tales the magnificent king makes an error or acts in a base manner and is turned into a beast, the handsome prince a frog, their high human cortex incorporated into their animal brains and lord help us. Or rather, Lady help us, the lord in such case being female, as those fairy tales point out. She alone, through her nurturing kiss and inherent wisdom, can bail the male out of the predicament his intellect constantly brings.
The Biology of Transcendence

Brain Growth Spurts and Shifts of Concentration of Development

The Model Imperative

The specific skills and capacities that emerge, from a wide spectrum of possibilities, do so in response to the states of relationship encountered at each stage. In *Magical Child,* and other works, this concept is referred to as the *model imperative*. Children develop only those capacities modeled by the adult culture. French-speaking mama,

French-speaking child is the classic example. For the early child, parents and adult culture *are* the environment. The model-environment expressed by adults is perceived and interpreted by the child from within their unique stage of development. A child may be very musical, innately, but as with any potential capacity, music must be modeled before it can be developed. The model imperative holds throughout life. As any parent or educator can testify, children become who we are, not what we tell them to be. To bring about a real change in development that change must be consistently modeled by the adult and the culture. Adults must become the change they wish to see in others, especially their own children. This is the model imperative and there is no exception.

Evolution - The Lower Into The Higher

Perception of self and other changes as we move from one developmental stage to another. Exploring and embodying the boundaries of each new stage brings about a fundamental change in our perception and interpretation of environmental signals. Each new stage draws up and transforms the previous into the service of the more complex and subtle realm now opening. Conception, pregnancy and childbirth, for example, represent a profound developmental experience. In this case the baby is the environmental signal that transforms development, physically, emotionally and often spiritually. Entirely new states of relationship and perception unfold, capacities which were unnecessary prior to conception. No baby, no need for the development of these stage specific capacities; the model imperative again.

Bonding during pregnancy or with a newborn baby transforms our perception of ourselves and our relationship to life. A bonded mother will risk her life to nurture and protect her crying baby. An unbonded mother may abuse her crying baby or abandon it all together. These are radically different responses to the same environmental signal. The difference is the interpretation of a given signal from two different points of view, bonded and unbonded. Being concerned for the well-being of others, affection, love and compassion are higher order responses, emanating from the forebrain. Concern for one's self, defensiveness and anger, are hindbrain responses. Development is transcendent. Bonding transforms the lower into the higher.

Schore describes how "shame is internalized and becomes the eye of the self looking inward... The other person, (the one originally inducing the shame) is then not needed... Shame becomes an imprint, a mental image of a misattuned mother face..." Such misatunement between infant-child and parent "engenders a rapid brake of arousal and the onset of an inhibitory state..." Inhibition is a form of depression, the same hormones are involved... The child develops awareness that an action they are about to take might bring painful emotional reactions. "Signal Shame" becomes the primary Model-Imperative, it blocks the child's natural acceptance of life, and introduces hesitancy and doubt. As the child moves out for some exploration-response, the signal from that "internal mentation is: Stop! You Are No Good. If You Do This, You Will Be Looked At And Despised."
The Biology of Transcendence

25

Devolution - The Higher Into The Lower

Nature fine-tuned her developmental stages over billions of years. She assumes a stable environment and opens each stage according to a well rehearsed biological schedule, regardless of geography or culture. A few hundred years ago technology began to radically alter the environment. Suddenly external signals failed to match nature's expectation, her biological timetable. Signals appropriate for later stages began flooding earlier stages. Anticipated, age and stage specific experiences were pushed aside by inappropriate challenges, which compromised the current stage at every level. Incomplete development of any early stage provides a weak foundation for everything that follows. Development stumbled and never fully recovered.

Nature strives for completion, for transcendence. Trauma at any stage compromises development. Attention which would normally go into learning and growth is shunted into defense. Rather than transcendence, compromised development demands that resources, which open at later stages, be used to fill in the gaps. Attempting to correct the error development takes a u-turn. Rather than higher capacities using and transforming lower energies, the lower use and transform the higher. Our high creative capacities are drawn into the service of the lower incomplete stages. The result is an extremely clever and creative, defensive, self-centered and aggressive population. Not a pretty sight. The solution is really quite simple, however: prevent the trauma by creating a safe, nurturing environment and by taking our cues from the child's innate intelligence rather than from corporate advertising on Saturday morning television.

Environmental Signals

The brain grows its structures in response to internal and external signals. The nature and quality of environmental signals determine the nature and quality of the capacities which are developed at each stage. Mother is the primary source of these signals for the early child. Her signals reflect her relationship to the environment, which includes her unborn or newborn baby. For 2,000 years the traditional Japanese culture surrounded pregnant mothers with safe, nurturing environments, a tradition called *Taikyo*. They knew long ago that the psychological and emotional state of the mother affects the baby's development.

Years ago research people discovered that the emotional state we are in when a learning takes place locks in as an integral part of that learning, not a footnote to it. We call this "state-specific" learning... The emotion experienced while leaning something is intricately associated with and part of the contents of the learned pattern. When we employ or exercise that learning, even years later, the same emotional hormones will fire in on cue, since they are as much a part of the neural pattern as any other material. And our body-brain-heart responds accordingly.
The Biology of Transcendence

New studies show that if a pregnant mother feels safe, her developing baby's forebrain, with its creative capacities, will be enhanced. If mother feels threatened, nature gives greater attention to the development of the baby's hindbrain, with its physical, survival, fight/flight, and sensory motor structures. When safe, nature puts her energy into creative growth. When threatened, nature defends herself.

States of Being & Their Meaning

State-Specific Learning

Feelings of safety or danger resonate throughout the entire body-mind as a state of being. In addition to stage-specific learning, researchers discovered that the emotional quality or state of an experience is recorded as part of the memory of that experience, a phenomenon known as "state-specific learning and performance." If learning $2 + 2 = 4$ was fun, for example, subtle feelings of play or joy will be experienced along with the next challenge to solve an equation. If learning to spell or trying out for Little League was humiliating, fear will be lurking in the background at the next spelling bee or athletic contest.

Jealousy is a state. Wonder is a state. Anger, rage, compassion, lust, joy, sadness, worry, love, fear, all are states—unique patterns of relationship. These states are changing all the time, and several may occupy us at the same time. We may be happy that our child is going off to college and sad that we will miss her company. As our outer and inner worlds change, so do our states. States have meaning. They contain information. Some states promote optimal learning and growth; others are more limiting. For the early child the information communicated in relationships *is* what he learns and what he remembers. The possibility of parenting in the Zone begins when adults discover they have a choice.

Research suggests that as much as 95 percent of all learning is state—specific. Only 5 percent of what we learn, lifelong, is acquired through formal instruction, training, or schooling. Of the 5 percent of information we learn through instruction, only 3 to 5 percent is remembered for any length of time. State-specific learning, what we refer to as "primary learning," is remembered for a lifetime. State-

Through the first brain we have present-tense only; through the second we have present and past. With the addition of the third brain we have awareness of past, present and future. And here evolution runs into a snag, even as she opens up a whole universe. The future introduces the issue of "what if the sun goes out"? Who has the flashlight?" Herein originates the possibility of useless anxiety and concern brought about by this forward-thinking intellectual brain, which as we have seen, can throw natures's high system into the service of the lower one. Anxiety induces that split of concentration found in a divided house. Anxiety can drive our highbrain to incorporate or join forces with our hindbrain. And with the incorporation of high forebrain into the service of hindbrain, we have a smart reptile on our hands, a danger to all.
The Biology of Transcendence

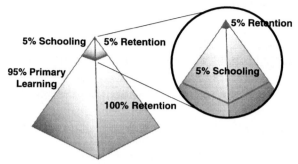

Lifelong Learning

specific learning and performance means simply that the quality of the state or relationship, as learning takes place, is woven into the memory of that experience.

Imagine, for example, a five-year-old boy learning to kick a soccer ball. Dad begins patiently by offering instruction on running, foot placement, ball alignment, spin, and velocity. Being less interested in performance than his well-meaning dad, the boy fails to reach or maintain the "expected" skill levels.

The boy would rather just play. Dad's state changes. He grows frustrated. His tone becomes focused, more intense. Sensing the tension, the boy's attention splits. Part of his attention goes into "trying" to kick the ball, the other part is channeled into defense. Performance plummets when attention splits. Dad yells. The boy cries. On a good day perhaps 3 to 6 percent of dad's verbal instructions will be remembered. The state-specific learning, the quality of the relationship, the disapproval and shame, may last a lifetime.

> Every organism responds to threat. Cells are intelligent. When there's poison in the womb, it's filled with alcohol or cocaine, the baby responds on a physical level. Early threats are like a knot in the beginning of a ball of yarn. The distortions caused by the knot get larger and larger as you wind more yarn onto the ball. The original experience that caused the knot may be very tiny, just a grain of sand, but it eventually ends up being pearl. As it grows the distortion is acted out in more sophisticated ways, as defense mechanisms, in patterns that please other people, in attitudes people think, feel and believe. These defense patterns often begin very early with just a little dab of terror, pain, or threat. People are shocked when

they discover how much these early impressions have affected their lives.

Personal Interview
Barbara Findeisen, M.F.C.C.
President, Association of Pre-& Perinatal Psychology and Health

Reflexes - Mental, Emotional, Physical Pinball

We are unaware of most of the activity taking place in our bodies and our minds each day. Much is governed by reflexes. Learning requires conscious awareness, attention, or intelligence. Reflexes don't. They are predetermined responses. Tap your knee just right, and it jerks mechanically in response to a given stimulus. David Bohm suggests that much of what we think and feel each day happens in the same way.

A human nurtured and not shamed and driven by fear develops a different brain and so mind, and will not act against the well-being of another, nor aganist his larger body, the living earth. As a child we know we are an integral part of the continuum of all things, as Jean Leidlofff explains and Jesus demonstrated. We can and must rediscover that knowing. Violent or repressive action against another is a projected form of suicide, and suicide is the solution to one denied love so completely as to lose all hope of ever attaining or knowing it. Three-year-olds commit suicide in the United States.
The Biology of Transcendence

> We can understand thought as a conditioned reflex. Take, for example, Pavlov and his dog. The dog has a natural reflex; it salivates when it sees food. If you ring a bell every time it sees food, the dog will associate the bell with the memory of perceiving food. Eventually it will skip the stage of perceiving food and salivate when the bell rings. I suggest that thought works in a similar way. When you think something, or have thought about something, it leaves a trace in memory and that trace reacts, according to the situation by association.

> We need repeated patterns clearly but the question is whether the repeated patterns dominate or whether something else comes in, something more intelligent. Perception has the ability to perceive something new, which is not contained in memory. The ability of repeated patterns to adapt to new circumstances is limited, they involve little or no intelligence. When thinking and thought become more and more automatic perception becomes less and less intelligent, less and less adapted to the particular situation. Very often people see so automatically that they hardly notice anything new. They tend to fall back into automatic reflexes.

Personal Interview
David Bohm, Ph.D.
Theoretical Physicist, Author, Educator

Beliefs, especially those we have about others and ourselves, operate like reflexes. Underneath them are assumptions. Assumptions live beneath the surface of our awareness. They predispose us to respond in predictable ways. Blondes are dumb. Jews are smart. Blacks are good athletes. Discovering that we are defined by reflexes most of the time is challenging enough. What is really embarrassing, if we still have a self-image to defend, is how very little intelligence there is in a reflex. Intelligence implies the attention and freedom to adapt appropriately to an ever-changing environment. Appropriate or intelligent means *a movement towards health and wholeness*. Predetermined responses lack this intelligence. Reflexes drive and determine a great deal of what we call parenting.

The *reflex system*, as Bohm calls it, predisposes us to behave in predictable patterns. They block all of the childlike qualities Ashley Montagu refered to as "growing young." Reflexes are great when driving freeways, but not so great when responding to children, who happen to be the most intelligent and dynamic learning systems in the known universe. Responding to their vast intelligence with predetermined, mechanical reflexes is not a good idea. How would you feel if a robot repeated over and over, "Take out the trash," "Clean up your room"? It is not the reflex that causes the trouble; it is the lack of attention and intelligence driving the reflex that does the damage.

When our attention is low the reflex system operates automatically. As attention increases our response to the world is more attuned to the present and potentially more intelligent, less reflexive. The greater the attention, the more potential intelligence we bring to the moment. The important factor is attention. Without attention, reflexes are the only response possible: they take over. With attention, reflexes become one of many possibilities. Giving attention to our state implies a shift out of reflexive patterns. In Optimum Learning Relationships, thought, feeling, and action are all responding withour conflict to the present moment. Reflexes may be involved but we are not limited to them. Attention transforms our experience.

The truth is, the fully conscious parent encompasses the psychological state of the child. They participate in shared functions that need no articulation, that simply call for spontaneous responses, a mutual meeting of needs and mutual fulfillment on emotional-intuitive levels.
Magical Child

The Magic of Memory

Our self-image is movement, like a flowing stream. Stop the flow and the image disappears. We often fail to see that the response that sustains our self-image is just that, a response. When the response becomes habituated, it creates the impression that there is a "thinker," a "me," some entity separate from the movement; from the response we call thought. The impression that there is a thinker causing all of our mental activity is part of the image-making nature of the brain/ mind. The movement of thought, which is more often than not reflexive, creates the image of a thinker. Thought, our self-image, and what we experience as the thinker are all the same movement. The millions and billions of contacts and connections that occur every day and their response create the image. The movement creates the thinker and the self-image, not the other way around.

Anxiety always cripples intelligence... Its roots are deep, its branches prolific, its fruit abundant, and its effects devastating.
Magical Child

For example, an impression from the external environment flows in: a sign along the road, the smell of jasmine in the evening air, a song on the radio; each impression may trigger a flood of memories. One memory triggers another and another. Memories are loaded with physical, mental, and emotional images and these flood the body and mind automatically. This same logic applies to our five-year-old, his well-intending dad and the soccer ball. No child chooses to feel bad about himself or herself. No one sets out to create a poor self-image. It happens naturally, automatically, in the mirror of relationship, just like the tears in our eyes when *that* song plays on the radio. Songs and tears are interdependent processes. So are little boys and girls, mothers and fathers.

The magic of memory occurs when a new contact triggers an instant replay of a previously learned event. This remembering floods the body with the mental, physical and emotional patterns associated with the original experience. The trigger point for this instant replay may be physical, such as a soccer ball. It may be emotional, like dad's frustration. It may be a word or phrase. Perhaps dad said something in his state of frustration. Any one of these associations can trigger an instant replay of the complete original pattern or *learned state* in the boy.

Learning research finds anxiety is the great enemy of intelligence and development. So its increase can be seen as an automatic index of a decrease in intelligence.
Bond of Power

Every time our five-year-old kicks a soccer ball he may stutter or stumble over earlier feelings of disapproval and shame associated with soccer balls, or any ball for that matter. His stuttering and stumbling increase the probability of future stumbling. This reinforces and validates the original state in which the learning took place. The ball was just one link, or doorway, to a state-specific learning pattern. Once this door is opened, the feelings of disapproval or shame from the original learning experience come pouring in. All of this happens so quickly and so automatically that we seldom catch the true source of our feelings. They sneak in beneath our level of awareness. Each time the boy approaches a ball this painful association may be repeated. Each time he feels the need to defend himself. Each defensive response is experienced as a self-image under attack. Soccer balls don't attack. There is in reality no threat, nothing to defend.

When watching a PGA tour player shake over a three-foot putt, Chuck Hogan, a sports performance specialist observed, "There's no dinosaurs on the golf course." The golfer's fear—and that of the little boy—are conditioned reflexes, shadows of some past experience being imagined in the present and projected into the future. Had that shameful memory not been recorded, all the energy and attention diverted to defense could have gone into learning and performance. Optimum is natural and easy when resistance to learning and performance is reduced or eliminated.

Two keys help to understand and eliminate these performance- robbing phantoms: awareness of the reflex and complete attention. The reflex pattern holds its power only as a reflex. Having an "insight," or seeing very clearly the nature of the pattern, breaks the pattern. Bringing greater attention to the moment also breaks the spell. When we give complete attention to the moment there is no energy remaining for defense. If attention is low, fear and defense can slip in. Attention is the critical and common factor. If both the child and adult are responding mechanically, reflexively, the old patterns will remain. The challenge rests with the adult. It is the adult who must see the nature of the reflex and bring increased attention to the state of their relationships. If the child had not been caught by the adult's false fears, he or she would not have created the defensive-image-reflex in the first place. The child would just kick the ball, watch it spin, adjust, and kick it again. Adults call this amazing process the Zone. Kids call it play.

The Primacy of States

It is not difficult to see that states are primary. They come first. New experiences are filtered through our current state. States have their own meaning, they contain their own information. They provide the context or reference needed to interpret our present experience.

Two closely bonded people often share information across time-space, to which we attach occultist labels of various sorts, while all the time it is only our true biology, the logic of our life system, the language of the heart.... Just as the intelligences drawn on by the brain lead to specific abilities, the heart draws on the supra-implicate order and realm of insight-intelligence (as described by Bohm). These higher orders don't articulate as specifics, but as general movement for the well-being and balance of the overall operations of the brain-mind.
Evolution's End

States affect what we see, what we remember, what we learn, and how we relate. How we relate translates into performance. How we perform is a reflection of our ease or *dis*-ease at this moment. If the challenge is mental, and the emotional experience is fearful, mental performance will be compromised. If the task is physical and the mental state is confused, physical performance will be impaired. States are primary.

In the right relationship, great performance flows naturally. Anxiety becomes a factor when we prejudge the outcome, when we focus on the score or grade instead of the challenge. Anxiety creates its own challenge in addition to kicking the ball. *Trying* to kick the ball is different from kicking the ball. Trying implies two things: attempting to kick the ball and compensating for being anxious. Compensating for anxiety reinforces anxiety. Trying harder makes things harder. The harder we *try*, the more we interfere and the greater our anxiety grows. It takes more and more energy to accomplish less and less. When challenged to save the Rebel Alliance, Luke Skywalker announced he would "try." Master Yoda replied, "Don't try. Do." Trying interferes. Just kick the ball.

States Are Content

Each state is a unique set of physical, emotional, and mental patterns, and each pattern affects our behavior. States of relationship are primary—they precede what we think of as content, learning, and performance. A broken leg or the flu, for example, are different physical states, yet each may cripple performance for an athlete or dancer. Anger, jealousy, and humiliation are different emotional states, and each affects differently how we think, feel, and behave. Listening or observing with great sensitivity, being confused, not knowing, or defending strong convictions are all states.

We are affected by and learn from the states of others. Sensing, responding to, and learning from the states of others occupy most of early childhood. That's what young children do. They participate in and learn from the information or meaning implicit in the adult state and this participation defines the early child. The adult state provides a context that gives order and meaning to the child's experience. The intimate learning that began before birth continues as children swim

Particles (and the universes built of them) being essentially light and variations on light, are subject to the speed of light as their ultimate limit of movement. On the other hand, the wave-fields from which they manifest are of a different state entirely, not "movement" or light but the frequency from which light itself springs, not in time-space, but the source of time-space. They are, in a word nonlocalized, whereas the particles they display are localized.
Evolution's End

in and learn from the presence of their parents, caregivers, and teachers.

Fields of Meaning

The meaning or information contained in a particular state may be compared to a *field* in quantum physics. Quantum fields are subtle, nonlocal patterns of pure energy. Unlike many traditional or Newtonian physicists, David Bohm believed that the universe is, in some way, conscious, and that this conscious energy is not confined by the boundaries that govern physical matter. The information, or meaning, implied in a field is everywhere, always, not limited by time or space. Bohm stated that it is not the intensity of a field but its form that gives it meaning. The meaning, form, or pattern of the field of subtle energy organizes physical matter. Bohm described how perception organizes matter—in this case you and me.

As long intuited, (by poet and saint) the fifth brain in our system lies in our heart... Neurocardiology, a new field of medical research, has discovered an actual, real and major brain center in our heart. And this heart-brain functions in dynamic with the fourfold brain in our head through a remarkable heart-head dynamic that is outside our conscious awareness. This dynamic reflects, affects and determines the nature of our resulting awareness itself, even as our awareness profoundly affects the heart-head dynamic in turn.
The Biology of Transcendence.

> The action depends only on the form of that field, not its intensity. Therefore it is not a mechanical action, like the wave pushing a cork or a ship around. It is more like a radar wave, which is guiding the ship on automatic pilot. The form (of the field) gives rise to the activity... In an ordinary state, for example, electrons are like a disorganized crowd of people. Electrons in a super-conduction state move in a regular, coordinated way, so they don't scatter. Now if you compare this to the ballet, you could say that the super-conduction state, the wave function, is like the score—it's kind of information—and the dance is the meaning of the score...To make this ballet dance analogy better, let's say the wave function is not fixed. The score depends on the initial configuration of the particles. The dance would vary according to the initial configuration of the dancers.

> David Bohm, Ph.D.
> In dialogue with Rupert Sheldrake
> *Dialogues with Scientists and Sages* by Renee Weber

The principles that govern electrons apply equally to large aggregates of electrons: you and me. The field generated by our state implies meaning or information. According to Bohm, the meaning of a field is in multidimensional space and operates, like radar, to organize matter, our body, for example. The meaning of a field is experienced and expresses from within rather than coming in through our physical senses. Intuition and telepathy are field effects. Remote viewing, precognition, and the direct "knowing" of the idio-savants (described in the opening chapters of *Evolution's End*), are all field effects. Particle patterns, what we call the physical universe, have meaning; they affect us. Wave or energy patterns also have meaning. They also affect us. We perceive, respond to, and learn from both energy and matter, though differently. State-specific learning and performance requires that we give attention to both dimensions, energy-mental and matter-physical, which we discover are, after all, two sides of the same coin.

Sharing Fields

Children and adults participate in common fields. Changing states imply changing patterns or meaning of the field. States are reciprocal and dynamic. A change in one person's state or field affects the other. This dynamic and reciprocal exchange of meaning is occurring all the time, everywhere. The unborn child, the infant, and the early child are extremely sensitive to field effects. They learn from them. Their radar is finely tuned. Intellectual and conditioned interference is low. Field resonance guides them, as much if not more, than the information gathered from their physical senses.

As we grow older, attention shifts from these inner fields of meaning to the images created by memory, thought, and imagination. Fields and their meanings are subtle. The inner imagery unfolding in the newer brain centers is spectacular by comparison. As the image-making capacity of the brain unfolds it overshadows the shared meaning of these field effects. As language and imagination develop, attention becomes enchanted by the flood of thought-forms and imagery created by the new brain. As a result, many adults miss this subtle resonance with young children. The child, however, does not.

The adult's local and nonlocalized states have meaning and represent vital information to the early child. The feeling or meaning of the adult's changing states resonates in these subtle fields, which expresses in the child as intuition or other subtle feelings. This inner nonverbal knowing provides the context, or filter, that gives order to the child's experience. When the inner state of the adult changes, so does the context for what the child learns. The quality of these first, primary

Long before it forms into our four-chambered thumper, our rudimentary heart furnishes the electromagnetic field surrounding the embryo from its beginning. This EM field is, in turn, encompassed by the mother's far more powerful heart field, as hers is nested in the earth and solar fields. One reason for the "in-arms" period is that the newborn infant requires this model, for the first months of life, just as with any other intelligent system. As was pointed out, close proximity with the mother's heart field stabilizes the infant's heart field.

The Biology of Transcendence

In 1983 John Hasted, physicist-mathematician at the University of London, published a study concerning dozens of children, averaging age nine, who could, given the right conditions, bend simple metal objects without touching them. In 1982, at the Monroe Institute in Virginia, twenty-five of us, ranging from five to seventy years, sat in a circle and, under the guidance of a United States Army colonel, bent stainless steel into various shapes by stroking it... A physicist at Melbourne University bent metal bars sealed inside glass cases. Spectrographs were made and demonstrated how steel, once bent in this fashion, had a chemical-molecular structure different from the same metal bent by mechanical pressure. In investigating the interaction of mind and matter, Robert Jahn found that ordinary people could influence electronic devices in classically "impossible" ways and stated that we must "rewrite the laws of physics."
Evolution's End

relationships establishes patterns of perception and behavior in the early child that last a lifetime. The state of the adult-child-relationship is infinitely more important than the information or skills we adults so urgently wish to convey or teach. States are primary. They impact learning, performance, and wellness, at any age.

The Intelligence of the Heart

A clear and present example of this field effect is the energy or intelligence of the heart. Quantum biologists describe a crystalline fluid structure in which the whole body is floating. Every part of the organism is in communication and in perfect resonance with every other part, and this inner symphony is orchestrated by the heart. New research shows that the frequencies and coherency of this liquid crystalline structure flows between people. These frequencies have meaning. They imply intelligence and information.

The emerging field of neurocardiology has discovered that up to 65 percent of the cells of the heart are neurons just like those found in

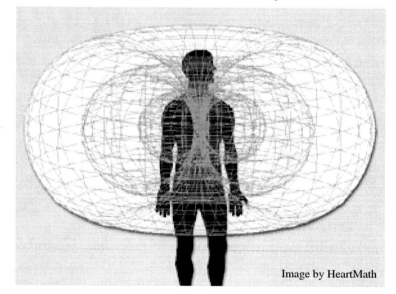

Image by HeartMath

the brain. John and Beatrice Lacey found, after thirty years of research for the National Institutes of Health, a direct unmediated neuro-connection, a direct pipeline, between the heart and the brain. The brain informs the heart of its general emotional state and the heart encourages the brain to make an intelligent response. Poets and sages have been saying this about the heart down through the ages. Neurocardiology and research at the Institute of HeartMath lift the intelligence of the heart out of poetry and poesy and into hardcore biology, where it belongs.

Each phase of the heartbeat creates its own part of the field effect that surrounds the body. The first is very short, close to the heart. The next radiates outward approximately three feet and is very powerful. The third field extends twelve to fifteen feet from the body.

It is easy to see that one person's field will often overlap another's. When two fields overlap they interact. This *resonant field effect* is present in every relationship, but is particularly important for mothers and infants. The meaning of the fields shared by mother and infant contain a great deal of critical information for both.

The importance of the field created by the heart is profound. David Bohm and other physicists describe how fields have meaning, how they imply information and intelligence. Much of the new research suggests that the heart field determines the general environmental conditions under which the genetic system spells out its instructions for new life.

It has been well known for many years that the mother's heartbeat has a profound effect on the growth of the fetus in the womb. Dr. Riddleston at Adelaide University in Australia was the first to claim that cellular imprinting of the mother's heartbeat began at conception and continued throughout the whole of development. Current research shows that the influence or intelligence of the heart covers many areas; hormonal, sound, electromagnetic and even more subtle field effects. The effect on the infant is wide-spread. Separating the infant from the mother breaks the *resonant field effect* they share. Separation causes the state of the infant's entire heart system to become unstable, incoherent, because it looses the stabilizing influence of the mother's heart field. Entrainment of the mother and infant's heart field is lost.

That heart fields entrain is a very precise, measurable, scientific fact. The amplitude and the Hertz value of the two heart frequencies become coherent. The waveforms match. When waveforms don't match we speak of dissonance. With entrainment there is no dissonance, no conflict. There is a state of harmony, wholeness and health.

Two poles of experience lie within us, our unique, individual selfgenerating through the brain, and a universal, impersonal intelligence generating through the heart. Success of human life depends on the development of this heart-mind dialogue... Since nature's model-imperative always holds, even a supreme intelligence must undergo development with us if we are to access and benefit from it. Unfortunately, no academic concept of a nurturing model-environment is provided for the "heart's intelligence," making our ignorance of it a dismal and crippling fact.
Evolution's End

When the infant's heart and the mother's heart are entrained, their brain structures also become synchronized. This entrained state keeps everything in balance and we refer to this entrained, balanced state as *bonding* between mother and infant. Later on this bonded state extends outward to include family, community and all of nature.

Failing the initial bond with the mother, all subsequent bonding is not only put at risk but is very difficult to bring about. The failure of a child to bond socially and become an active member of the society is not the child's moral or ethical failure. It is the failure to establish, in the beginning, that bond upon which the later social bonds must be built. Studies at Harvard University show clearly that the nature of our early bonds are reflected throughout life, both in one's health and ability to interact socially. Allan Schore describes how the first eighteen months of life determine the subsequent moves of the intelligence and capacities to relate for the rest of one's life. Why? Because the emotional experience the child is given during the first eighteen months of life determines the nature and quality of the neural structures that develop in that period. Schore traces all the pathologies in teenagers and adults back to the failure of appropriate emotional nurturing during the first eighteen months of life. Emotional nurturing translates directly into the field effect—shared or not shared—with the immediate environment. During those first eighteen months that environment is mother, father, and other primary caregivers.

Our intellectual creative brain is critically dependent on the emotional system. Cognition is limited by the nature and development of our emotional system. If we want to develop higher levels of intelligence, in ourselves and in our children, we must first develop our emotional intelligence, or we have no foundation to move on into the higher levels of human intelligence. It is on this very basis that our educational and family systems are falling apart. We are not furnishing the fundamental foundation of emotional security, the safe space, and the bonding early in life. And this emotional nurturing again is determined by the coherency or the incoherence of the heart fields we all share, but especially between mother and infant. This entrained emotional bond provides the necessary foundation for the higher intelligence to unfold. If we want brilliant children, we must honor and follow the intelligence of the heart right from the beginning.

Full development, for which we are genetically equipped, is pure creativity, which can only take place by thought being developed as an instrument of insight-intelligence, open to and capable of handling the awesome power of consciousness. Anything less is incomplete development, which will always (no matter how much gadgetry we pile around us) cause anxiety because we aren't developing the higher levels of abstract or non-physical thought we must have for "mental autonomy." Autonomy is the ability to create a perceptual experience not dependent on our given physical materials, even though our creative ability must arise out of those given materials.
Bond of Power

Insight-Intelligence and Beginner's Mind

The meaning or information embodied by the heart, and other fields, is blocked by everyday thinking. When challenged, the brain's associative process sorts through its database of experiences and proposes a response based on what is known. Most of us spend most of our days and nights in the state of mind we call "thinking" with its worrying, planning, projecting, and controlling. Thinking and thought are essentially and almost exclusively self-generative. That is, the source or raw materials used in the process we call thinking is already known. Thinking and thought involve memory and memory is the past, that which is known. We can imagine and dream of new possibilities but the context or source for these creations is already known; it preexists.

Real learning and real relationship occur in what Yogic philosophy calls the *eternal present*. Learning and relationship may include the past but can not be defined or limited exclusively by the past. To do so would exclude the intelligence being expressed in this present, creative moment. True adaptive learning and real relationship, as opposed to reflexive conditioning, involve a constant merging of the unknown-present with the known-past. What we know is constantly being transformed by what we do not know.

The source of the intelligence and information conveyed by the heart, and other field effects is not found in memory. The information implied in fields, as described by David Bohm and others, is accessible only in the present. The meaning of a field expresses or displays in perception as *flashes of insight*. We might compare insight to the unlearned knowing of the idio-savant, or the sudden *Eureka!* discoveries of Einstein and others. To be open to insight the doors of perception must open; not be blocked or limited by what is already known. Zen philosophy calls this free and receptive mental state *beginner's mind*.

In the life-and-death situation, sword tip to sword tip with the enemy, where should the swordsman put his mind? Should he think about the latest fad in sword swinging? Should he ponder what his mother might think of his soiled sandals? While zooming toward the Death Star, Obi-Wan Kenobe whispered nothing to Luke about the sophisticated gadgetry on board the X-Wing. "Use the Force, Luke," was all

Nature programs the child to do two things from ages one to seven; structure a knowledge of the world exactly as it is, on the one hand , and play with that world in ways that it is not, on the other...
New patterns for sensory organization and bodily action form in the child's brain only as s/he interacts with the world though the body. Throughout childhood, a full-dimensional and accurate concept (structure of knowledge) is an internalization of an external act.
Magical Child

he said. "Use the force" might be translated into "Stop looking in the rearview mirror, at the past, in hopes of meeting this present challenge. Don't focus exclusively on imagined outcomes and allow the fields of intelligence resonating in and around you right now to express through you."

As the beginner knows nothing about either his body posture or the positioning of his sword, neither does his mind stop anywhere within him. If a man strikes at him with the sword, he simply meets the attack without anything in mind. As the beginner studies various things and is taught the diverse ways of how to take a stance, the manner of grasping his sword, and where to put his mind, his mind stops in many places. Now if he wants to strike at an opponent, he is extraordinarily discomforted. Later, as days pass in accordance with his practice, neither the postures of his body nor the ways of grasping the sword are weighted in his mind. His mind simply becomes as it was in the beginning, when he knew nothing.

Takuan Soho
Sixteenth Century Writings of the Zen Master to the Sword Master
The Unfettered Mind, Translated by William Scott Wilson

Attention is required for learning any new skill. We become what captures our attention. Like a lens, attention channels energy. The focus of energy through the lens of attention forges new brain development. The more complete the attention, the more energy is focused and the greater the learning and corresponding brain development. Optimum states of learning and performance make optimum use of attention. Are we meeting the moment with complete attention? Is our focus of energy unconflicted? Or, is some attention being held in reserve, just in case we have to defend our self-image? At Play or in the Zone, especially in relationship with children, the quality of our attention makes all the difference.

If you put your mind in your right hand, it will be taken by the right hand and your body will lack its functioning… If you don't put it anywhere it will go to all parts of your body and extend throughout its entirety.

Takuan Soho
Sixteenth Century Writings of the Zen Master to the Sword Master
The Unfettered Mind, Translated by William Scott Wilson

"Use the Force, Luke," was a reminder to release the mind from the concentration camp of the intellect and its well-armed defenses. *Flow* is this state of the beginner's mind, where "mind" or "attention" expands naturally throughout the entire body and beyond, inviting the unknown to express its intelligence, in and through us, right now.

Our goal is to apply the principles of "state-specific learning and performance" (being in the Zone, Flow and original Play), to parenting and to education. Years of research from diverse fields reveal a dramatic new approach to human development. Extraordinary is built into every cell of our body. Optimum is nature's baseline for learning, performance, and wellness. Miracles happen every day when resistance to learning, peak performance and well-being is reduced or eliminated. Optimum is completely natural. It is easy, as easy as child's play. In fact, it is play.

Original Play—The Optimum State

The Intelligence of Play

Battling the Evil Empire and life-and-death bouts with swords are dramatic. They are exceptions to the normal run of life. Being in the Zone, that Optimum Learning Relationship, means being fully aware, alive, and engaged in this precious moment and all its relationships. And what do most animals and humans do when they feel safe and nurtured, when they are in the state of *Flow*? They "play" hide-and-go-seek, chess, cards, and baseball. They play with the dog, pretend, and ponder. Play is not the activity however; play is a state, a unique quality of relationship.

What we do in the play state changes with our age and stage of development. Michael Jordan has this special relationship with basketballs. Writers and poets have playful relationships with words. Musicians play with sounds. Singers and actors play with emotions. Einstein played with ideas. Children play with anything they can, and especially with the people they love. Nature set aside all of childhood to explore and develop this unique and very special relationship called play.

Play states are now seen as the major driving force in the develop-

Anxiety can only breed anxiety. Anxiety is the one condition intolerable to us. And thought generated by anxiety, even though the impulse is to escape anxiety, will always relate to, and have inherent within, that anxiety. Isolated thought can't give unity, and only in unity are we free from anxiety... When our eye is on error, we become that error. Like attracts like. Error produces error.
Bond of Power

41

ment of higher brain function. The greater the intelligence of the species, the more they play. The greater the skill of the player in nature, the larger and more intricate is their brain. Human play, like the play of animals, is necessary for optimal brain development, socialization, flexibility, and adaptability. Real play is how real learning and real development takes place. It is that simple. John Douillard describes the importance of original play and its affect on the performance of elite athletes.

> If you talk to elite athletes, and I've coached many of them, they say the same thing. "My best race was my easiest race." When Roger Bannister broke the four-minute mile he said, "The world seemed to stand still. I felt like I was running slow. I felt no pain and no strain." And he was running faster than any man alive. When Billy Jean King was at her best, she would transport herself beyond the turmoil of the court to a place of total peace and calm. Look at the Tarahumara Indians who run 75 to 150 miles a day, and kick a little ball the whole way; it's a game. After running a 26-mile run, they finished with blood pressures lower when than when they started. Their breath rate was what we would consider normal at rest, and they were running an 8-minute mile pace the whole way, at high altitudes. To them it was fun, a way of life. One hundred fifty miles in a day is a lot of activity but their experience is one of calm. They love it so much that they slip easily and naturally into a place to where peak performance flows automatically. It's not stressful. It's not work. It's play.

Personal Interview
John Douillard
Author, *Body, Mind & Sport*

Play is the foundation of creative intelligence, but like any intelligence, it must be developed, in keeping with nature's model imperative, the child who is played with will learn to play. The child who is not played with will be unable to play and be at risk on every level.
Evolution's End

Play As Learning

Most adults have it backwards. They think that learning is serious and that play is unimportant, a waste of time. True play optimizes and expands learning, performance, and wellness. Other states; concentration, competition, the pressures imposed by rewards and punishments, limit growth to predefined patterns. Learning becomes mechanical, rote, and conditioned. The intelligence of play is lost when relationships become automatic, reflexive.

Intelligence embraces. It is a movement toward wholeness and well-being. Play takes the lid off learning by returning the body and mind to their natural order. Resistance is reduced, opening possibilities few have ever imagined.

The adult mind has been adulterated, contaminated by years of conditioning. With the best of intentions, adults impose this conditioning on children. Adults worry. Is my child measuring up to standards? Is he or she sitting up, learning to walk, talking, riding a bike, hitting the ball, dancing as well as other children? Does my child have what it takes to pass the SAT? Comparison, competition, rewards, and punishments place false and unnecessary limitations on learning and performance, crippling true development.

The Zone, that optimum state of flow, occurs naturally when all three levels of the brain—thought, feeling, and action—are focused on a particular activity. This complete attention cannot occur if we feel threatened in any way. Are we being graded? Will we measure up to standards? Are we to be punished or rewarded?

Competition prevents optimum learning and performance. We can not gather and focus all our attention. We think, I'd better do this; and if I can't, I'll catch it, I'll be a failure, a loser. I'll be punished or rejected. Fear and conflict prevent the body from acting on its own wisdom. We are a house divided against ourselves and there is no health in us, no wholeness. As a result, no concentrated learning or performance can take place. When we feel safe, thought, feeling, and action are free to playfully explore our universe. Real learning takes place in what Maria Montessori called "the absorbent mind of the child." Children given a safe and nurturing setting simply absorb their universe. They absorb it and become it, and they do this through play.

Play develops intelligence, integrates our triune nature; prepares us for higher education, creative thought, and helps us prepare for becoming an effective parent when that time comes. Play is the very force of society and civilization, and a breakdown in the ability to play will reflect in a breakdown of society.
Evolution's End

Authentic Play Defined—Well Almost

It is difficult for many adults to appreciate the importance of play. Most adults lost touch with this magical state years ago. Before exploring how play transforms our approach to parenting and to education, let's look at this optimum state from three perspectives, that of educator/researcher, scientist, and explorer.

The Researcher

In 1990 Mihaly Csikszentmihalyi published *Flow, the Psychology of Optimal Experience*. The book summarizes decades of research on the most positive aspects of human experience—joy, creativity, the process of total involvement in life and its relationships. The author explains:

> Optimal experience is an end in itself… it is a self-contained activity, one that is not done with the expectation of some future benefit, the doing itself is the reward.

> Flow lifts the course of life to a different level. Alienation gives way to involvement, enjoyment replaces boredom, helplessness turns into a feeling of control, and psychic energy works to reinforce the sense of self, instead of being lost in the service of external goals. When experience is intrinsically rewarding, life is justified in the present, instead of being held hostage to a hypothetical future gain… The solution is to gradually become free of societal rewards and learn how to substitute for them rewards that are under one's own powers.

> Concentration is so intense that there is no attention left over to think about anything irrelevant, or to worry about problems. Self-consciousness disappears, and the sense of time becomes distorted. An activity that produces such experiences is so gratifying that people are willing to do it for its own sake, with little concern for what they will get out of it, even when it is difficult or dangerous.
>
> Mihaly Csikszentmihalyi
> *Flow, the Psychology of Optimal Experience*

Play is the universal characteristic in all the young of all higher species. Because the economy of nature rules out random or wasted action in the formative period, the child's driving intent to play all the time must logically be a major part of the biological plan.
Magical Child

Most parenting and education models are based on conditioning, external rewards, and punishments. These control strategies reduce learning and performance to predetermined patterns. Learning becomes reflexive, repetitive, mechanical. A predetermined response to fresh challenges lacks the dynamic flexibility of true intelligence. Conditioning introduces potential failure, the implied threat of possible public humiliation and censure. With conditioning, the optimal experience found in real Play, Flow, or the Zone is denied.

Truly great performance is achieved when the body, mind, and emotions are in complete alignment, when total participation in the experience is its own reward, when we are psychologically free of defensive doubts and anxieties—all of which unfold naturally when one feels related and safe.

The Scientist

David Bohm knew very well that creative inquiry, which is the heart and soul of science, is play.

> The essential activity of science consists of thought, which arises in creative perception and is expressed through play. This gives rise to a process in which thought (and experience) unfolds into provisional knowledge, which then moves outward into action and returns as fresh perception and knowledge. This process leads to continuous adaptation of knowledge, which undergoes constant growth, transformation, and extension. Knowledge is therefore not something rigid and fixed that accumulates indefinitely in a steady way, but is a continual process of change. Its growth is closer to an organism than a data bank. When serious contradictions in knowledge are encountered, it is necessary to return to creative perception and free play, which act to transform knowledge. Knowledge, apart from this cycle of activity, has no meaning… When creativity is made subservient to external goals, which are implied by seeking rewards, the whole activity begins to degenerate.
>
> David Bohm, Ph.D. and F. David Peat, Ph.D.
> *Science, Order & Creativity*

Play creates a new and flexible relationship with experience and with knowledge. Knowledge never becomes absolute; is never unyielding. This includes all the theories, beliefs, ideas, images, and opinions we have about ourselves, and others, especially our children. Knowledge, including our beliefs about parenting and education, becomes "provisional." Being temporary constructs, rather than fixed and absolute, the knowledge we gather in play is constantly open for renewal. As Bohm described: *Knowledge then moves outward into action and returns as fresh perception and knowledge. This process leads to continuous adaptation of knowledge, which undergoes constant growth, transformation, and extension.*

The Explorer

O. Fred Donaldson, Ph.D., a play explorer, educator, and author of the Pulitzer-nominated book, *Playing By Heart,* describes the unique quality of relationship found in optimum experience.

> Original play is both an all-embracing vision of reality and a practice of kindness which permeates all of one's relationships. To play in this way is to be in touch and to be touched deeply by our authentic human nature and the natural world. Original play culti-

Insight seems a "grace," which is freely given rather than made by our effort. Einstein spoke of his insight arriving like a flash of lightning which, though they lit up the landscape of his mind for only an instant, forever after changed its landscape. The only thing which can change the nature of our thought is an energy more powerful than thought.
Bond of Power

Anxiety is not some passing emotional disturbance, but a biological imbalance flashing in its danger-to-survival signals. The result of anxiety is (in a technological society), an increased demand for the production of technological "advances" to "extend our powers" and so relive that anxiety. This creates a neat, double-bind vicious circle since the end-result is always greater loss of personal power, more anxiety and more demand for further gimmickry.
Bond of Power

vates an ever-renewing sense of enchantment and engagement with the world. It develops calmness, awareness, and a flexible ability to handle stress, surprise, or challenges without aggression. This play develops radically different behaviors than those encouraged by the dominant contest culture. The response is deeper, more universal, and authentic. When we are in this state of original play, the limitations of our cultural identity drop away. Original play is truly an ecological intelligence. The sensitivity this play develops needs to be understood and integrated into all aspects of family, community, and professional life. Discovering the intelligence of play opens once again the genius of childhood most of us lost long ago.

O. Fred Donaldson, Ph.D.
Essay on Play as Belonging

The Mystic

We began our exploration with Michael Murphy's description of transcendent experiences in sports.

The great seers of the contemplative traditions have explored the inner life more deeply than most of us, and they have opened up spiritual territories that we may or may not enter. But many athletes and adventurers have followed partway, however inadvertently, through the doorways of sport.

Michael Murphy, Rhea A. White
In the Zone, Transcendent Experiences in Sports

The state we call Play, the Zone, or Flow *is* transcendent. Play transcends the current set of boundaries we find ourselves in, at any age, stage or activity. The goal is always to reach beyond, to expand the limitations of known boundaries. To do so we must leave behind or at least temporally suspend the boundaries imposed by our social and cultural identity. Optimum Learning Relationships are transcendent. Being free from the blinders imposed by our conditioning—personified as personal identity—the quality and nature of all relationships expand. When the boundaries of "me" expand or disappear—that center which we defend so passionately—what remains is our true nature, vast and indescribable. O. Fred Donaldson describes this experience as belonging. The educator and philosopher J.Krishnamurti, close friend of Bohm, described this mystical absence of this defensive self-image as choiceless awareness, true freedom and real intelligence.

When you are completely attentive, there is no self, no limitation.

Krishnamurti, Washington DC, 1985

When you give complete attention, with all the energy that one has, fear completely disappears.

Krishnamurti, Ojai, California, 1981

So long as there is a center [a self image] creating space around itself there is neither love or beauty. When there is no center and no circumference, then there is love. When you love, you *are* beauty.

Krishnamurti, *Freedom From the Known*

When you see the extraordinary beauty of the earth, its rivers, lakes, mountains, [or your child], what actually takes place? At that moment the very majesty of the mountain makes you forget yourself. You don't exist, only that grandeur exists. Beauty is, where you are not.

Krishnamurti, Madras, India 1982

The children were playing about, but they never looked at that lovely spring day. They had no need to look, for they *were* spring. Their laughter and their play were part of the tree, the leaf, and the flower. You felt this, you didn't imagine it. It was as though the leaves and the flowers were taking part in the laughter, in the shouting, and in the balloon that went by. Every blade of grass, the yellow dandelion, and the children were part of the whole earth. The dividing line between man and nature disappeared; but the man on the race-course in his car and the woman returning from the market were unaware of this. Probably they never looked at the sky, at the trembling leaf, the white lilac. There were carrying their problems in their hearts, and the heart never looked at the children or the brightening spring day. The pity of it was that they breed these children and the child would soon become the man on the race-course and the women returning from the market; and the world would be dark again. Therein lay the unending sorrow. The love on the leaf would be blown away in the coming autumn.

Krishnamurti, *The Only Revolution*

As any botanist or biologist (or gardener) will tell you, an organism threatened continually in its early formative period tends to reproduce quickly. The child's nature gets the message that we are not long for this world, so lets make sure at least our species survives. Thus sexual maturation speeds up dramatically. A group of medical doctors in upstate New York found a direct correspondence between early menses, television viewing, and general stress-anxiety. Thus upwards of 24% of American female children, seven years of age, now develop breasts, begin menses at eight, and pregnancies are now epidemic at nine. The same sexual precocity takes place in boys.
The Biology of Transcendence

Safe Enough To Play

The Safe Place

Freedom implies safety. The greater the sense of safety, the greater

47

the play and the more dynamic learning becomes. Introduce fear of any kind, and development falters. Defense strategies kick in—flight/fight, comparison, competition, striving for rewards and avoiding punishments. Learning becomes defensive. The greater the fear the greater the demand for protection, which often leaves very little energy for growth and development.

Cellular biologist Bruce Lipton, reporting on new genetic research, confirms that states of perception are stronger predictors of results than *actual reality*. The body organizes for protection or growth depending on one's *interpretation* of environmental cues. Perceived danger affects the body even if the danger is imaginary. Changes in perception, or state, affect both the context and content of any learning experience, and this translates directly into how we develop as human beings.

Intellect, driven by novelty, asks only, "Is it possible?" Intelligence, driving for our well-being and fulfillment, asks, "Is it appropriate?" A fully developed and integrated intellect could not, by its nature, make any move that was not for the well-being of self, society, and world. We would, by the very nature of our minds, be incapable of dumping 100 million tons of violently toxic chemical waste on our own nest, or spend enough on armament in a day to adequately feed the seven million or so children who starve to death each year.
Evolution's End

> The research community recently confirmed that changes in the environment can modify our genes. In terms of development, the environment suddenly became more important than genes. It's not simply the environment, but our interpretation of the environment that makes the critical difference.
>
> The body is designed to fluctuate between growth and protection depending on how it interprets the environment.
> When we feel safe and loved, the switch says we're in a growth mode. If the environmental signals are interpreted as threatening, we go into a protection mode. When the switch goes from growth to protection, growth is compromised.
>
> In the fifties for example, people had bomb shelters for protection. But they didn't live in the shelter. They lived and grew outside. When the sirens went off, they went down into the shelter for protection. But how long can you stay in the bomb shelter? The protection provided by the shelter was intended only for a short period. Trying to live in the protection mode compromises growth. Pretty soon you're out of food, out of water, out of air, and then you're dead. Every cell in our body reacts the same way....As we start to perceive the environment as being hostile, less than safe, less than loving, the system will automatically shift into protection to protect its survival. The more chronic the protection, the less growth there is.

Personal Interview
Bruce Lipton, Ph.D.
Cellular Biologist

Children are compelled by nature to embrace and explore their world. This exploration, shaped by their early relationships with parents and the natural world, creates neural networks, or protein filters, which evolve into worldviews. Worldviews are life-long patterns that predetermine how we interpret the world and its relationships.

If there is no safe place to play, children can not trust the world they are trying to embrace. Children will look at the world as the enemy and build a defense against it. This will reduce their sensory intake from that world dramatically. Anxiety-ridden children—those suffering psychological abandonment—have a sensory intake of 25 to 30 percent less than children who are given emotional nurturing. Maria Montessori speaks of the child coming into the world as an absorbent mind, ready to expand and embrace the universe within, to utilize fully all their genetically inherited capacities. If the child is not given a safe space, if the child is damaged or traumatized, he or she will close into a tight defense against a world that cannot be trusted. This reduced sensory intake seriously impairs neural development and *results in completely different structures of knowledge.*

Optimum Learning Relationships unfold naturally when we feel safe and connected. When we feel safe, connected, bonded, we play with our world and all its relationships. If we don't feel safe, an internal switch is flipped and we become protective, defensive. At every moment we have these two possibilities; the direction taken profoundly affects how we interpret the world, what we learn, how well we perform and our general feeling of health or *dis*-ease. Denied emotional nurturing or a safe space, a child's higher intelligences will be limited, constrained, and impaired, and the capacities that *are* developed will be used to strengthen their defense against the world. The child who is given a safe, nurturing environment—where he or she need not defend against the world—will embrace and explore their world. For the emotionally safe child there is a constant expansion of potential, capacity, and possibility from lower intelligences into higher and higher intelligences—the intelligence of play in action.

Marshall Klaus of Case Western Reserve Hospital in Cleveland, Ohio makes the astonishing claim that if properly bonded with the mother, the child should never cry. Crying, he states, is an unnatural, abnormal, uncommunicative expression, an emergency distress mechanism only. And in those societies where bonding is practiced, crying is, indeed quite rare. Other forms of communication are used, and these infants and children develop senses of personal power such responsiveness give... they have a matrix from which to operate.
Magical Child

At birth the baby has moved from a soft, warm, dark, quiet and totally nourishing place to a harsh sensory overload. S/he is physically abused, violated in a wide variety of ways, subjected to specific physical pain, and insult, all of which could still be overcome, but s/he is then isolated from his/her mother... This isolation neatly cancels every possible chance for bonding, for the relaxation of the birth stress, for activation of the sensory systems for its extrauterine function, and for the completion of the reticular formation for full mental-physical coordinates and learning. The failure to return to the known matrix (mother) sets into process a chain reaction from which the organism never fully recovers. All future learning is affected. The infant body goes into shock. The absorbent mind shuts down... Stage specific processes, once missed, must be laboriously rebuilt.
Magical Child

Basic Trust

Basic trust implies that children and adults experience the world as being safe. A lack of basic trust means that the world and its relationships must be defended against. Feeling physically and emotionally safe with mom, dad, and other primary caregivers, during the critical early years, creates a physical and emotional foundation of basic trust. Participating in safe, nurturing relationships with adults, children learn to trust themselves in those relationships. Feeling safe, they venture into, encounter, embrace, and embody their world, which for the early child is ever new and challenging. Jean Leidloff discovered the importance of basic trust in the Amazon jungle.

It was quite an experience for a sheltered Manhattanite, hiking through the jungle, meeting snakes and scorpions, sleeping in a hammock. The people we encountered were living in the Stone Age. It was not the diamonds I came home talking about; it was the Indians and how they lived, what kind of lives they had and what the children were like. It became clear that we have made a terrible mistake about human nature. We are under the misapprehension that we're born bad, or in the official words of the Church of England, innately depraved, and that is simply not true.

I was living for more than two years with these Indians, looking straight at them and not really seeing them, because I was so blinded by preconceptions. I didn't even notice that, amazingly, the children never fought. They played together all day unsupervised, all ages, from crawling, to walking to adolescence. Not only did they not fight, they never even argued. This is not at all what we have been taught human nature is—boys will be boys. So I thought well maybe, boys won't be boys.

One thinks well, these are savages. They wear red paint and feather loin cloths, so they are not people. But they are exactly the same species as we are, except they are behaving the way we all evolved to behave. We, on the other hand, are mistreated as infants and children, treated inappropriately for our species.

As a result, we keep re-creating an anti-social population. Nobody's born rotten. You just don't have bad kids. It's not true. There is no such thing. But we can make them bad.

Just imagine the neurotic and psychopathic people that we have become. Why do we have a 50% divorce rate? Why do we have so many police? It's not just Americans, it's the whole of western civilization laboring under a misapprehension of what human nature truly is.

Researchers faithfully try to document what is *normal*. Nobody I know really wants a normal child. Just look at normal. It includes what's called the terrible twos, which are sort of wild, bossy tantrum-prone con-men. Luckily they're small otherwise we'd really be in trouble. And we've got God knows what kinds of drudgery and alienation for children and parents.

We use the word *normal* as though it were a synonym for *natural*, which it is not. Normal is how we *think* children must be. This includes things like three month colic, where babies are constantly vomiting. They call it spitting up so it doesn't sound like a real illness, but it is an illness. It's painful. This happens even when babies are drinking their mother's milk. They're throwing up.

How can we believe that we alone evolved over millions of years without being able to digest our own mother's milk? Why are *normal* babies so stressed that they can't keep their food down? The babies I saw in the jungle never had indigestion unless they were ill with a fever. Babies never threw up. They were not wriggling and struggling and arching and flexing and squeaking like ours do *normally*. So normal is adversarial. I hope people realize that what they're doing with all the love in their hearts, and I have no doubt of that, *is* adversarial.

When you're following the advice of the doctors or the experts or your mother-in-law, your mother or your sister or whomever; when you are feeding the baby on a schedule, denying it physical contact, not allowing it to sleep with you and be with you, twenty-four hours a day, not less, then you're being adversarial.
It's perfectly clear that the millions/billions of babies, who are crying at this very moment, want unanimously to be next to a live body. Do you really think they're all wrong? Theirs is the voice of nature. This is the clear pure voice of nature, without intellectual interference.

Whatever children are doing—is learning. They're learning like little sponges, all the time. But they're told, "Stop it because this is

The intelligence of the heart is not some sweet sentiment but a primary biological necessity and the foundation of all bonding. Bonding itself develops in clear stages: mother-infant, infant-family, family-society, and a final male-female "pair-bonding" on which life itself is based. This series of biological links is the primary job of the first level of heart intelligence, and far more powerful stages lie in wait, contingent on the successful completion of this first major stage.
Evolution's End

worthless. What is important is this. Pay attention. 'A' is for apple." Everything else is undermined and pronounced worthless. All your authority figures tell you that your nature, which is to explore, is worthless. If *they* don't *teach* you, it's not learning. I've recently come to the startling but obvious conclusion that learning occurs naturally, but teaching isn't natural at all. I can't remember ever seeing any of the people I'm talking about, who live so successfully, *teaching*. The little ones are learning from the older children or from the adults, but nobody's teaching. They're learning on their own initiative, which is so powerful. You don't have to augment it. In fact you can't really augment it. There's no way you can make a child learn better than he would if he or she wants to.

By the time we have our first child, we're so conditioned not to believe our innate feelings that we have total strangers in the hospital tell us what to do and we don't know any better. It's tragic. We have an exquisitely evolved innate knowledge of how to do things. Mothers know that the baby should not be taken away at birth but they have been so conditioned to believe in an *authority* and not themselves, that they deny their own wisdom.

We've described normal. Let's contrast it with examples of what you would consider natural. The baby knows what it needs, and the minute you put it down, it cries. It's letting you know. It's signaling you perfectly clearly, "don't put me down!" And we have built into us equally, without a dictionary, the knowledge of what it means when the baby goes "waa, waa, waa." We know it means, "pick me up. Don't put me down. Don't leave me!"

Until very recently doctors routinely performed operations on babies without anesthesia. The baby screams but the trained professionals deny it feels pain! How can mothers deny their own innate wisdom? How can we have drifted so far off?

Personal Interview
Jean Leidloff
Author of <u>The Continuum Concept</u>

The first hour after birth is the most critical time in human life. For now the bond is established in strange, mysterious and unfathomable ways. Anyone else around literally gets caught in the magnetic fields of attraction weaving back and forth. A great love affair is being born, a love affair that is sensuous, sexual, spiritual, mental and quietly ecstatic. As Marshall Klaus put it, "they must learn to make love with each other." ...Only in the great second bonding, many years hence, will life again enter into this same ecstasy.
Magical Child

A Lifetime of Experience in a Glance

When new experiences arise, and they always do, children glance at mom or dad to reaffirm their safe place. The adult's return glance communicates two things: First, it reestablishes the bond and confirms a worldview of basic trust. Second, the child's glance implies a question. What's that? The adult's perception of the object the child is about to encounter brings about a change in the adult. A child about to reach for a scorpion will elicit a very different response, or field effect, from the adult than if the child were reaching for a fuzzy caterpillar. The act of perception in the adult changes the meaning of their state. The adult's personal knowledge and experience with the object resonates through the relationship. Trusting the relationship, the child responds accordingly, which builds greater trust in the relationship. This cycle repeats with every new encounter. If the child feels safe, protected, each playful encounter reinforces his or her worldview of basic trust. Their world and capacity to embrace the world expands. "For he who has," the Bible notes, "more is given."

The Learning Channel We Call Bonding

Almost everyone has heard the term *bonding*, coined years ago by John Kennel and Marshall Klaus, to describe the intimate connection found between mothers and their newborn babies. The term, however, is misleading. To bond is to join, glue, tie, or connect together two separate objects. Again, O. Fred Donaldson describes this state of relationship as *belonging*, which means to fit in, or to be in the right place. Connecting two separate objects is much different than affirming unity. We need to bond only when there has been a separation. Belonging is more expansive, dynamic, and inclusive.

We *are* relationship, whether we call it bonding, belonging, connection, attachment, or communion. *The meaning, or information implicit in our relationship changes moment by moment.* What we call learning is discovering and exploring a particular set, or pattern, of relationships. The stove is hot, is a relationship. The bee stings, water is wet, aunt Molly brings presents, honey is sweet, all describe states of relationship. And that is what we learn. Bonding therefore is much more than sweet sentiment. Bonding is a channel of communication, information and shared meaning.

We may belong in a particular environment, and relate to many wonderful things, dogs and cats, brothers and sisters, turtles and toys. One relationship, however, is more important than the rest. The relationship between mother and baby, or father and baby provides the *context*, or reference, for all the other relationships. The adult-child

To take part in society we must accept the social definitions and agreements that make up society's reality picture. Our definitions outline the socially acceptable framework for what shall be considered real. This network definition changes from culture to culture and period to period. It is arbitrary to an indeterminable degree, but is always the only reality available... Our culture and our reality are not separate phenomena.
Crack in the Cosmic Egg

bond ensures an open, constant, and dynamic channel of communication. Information is constantly flowing through this learning channel we call bonding.

This critical flow of communication between the early child and caregivers requires three things. First, the adult must be physically present. Second, the adult must be aware of what the child is experiencing. Third, the child must be aware of the adult's changing relationship to the world they share. This physical connection and shared awareness creates a constant flow of communication that changes instant-by-instant, encounter-by-encounter, throughout the day.

Consider how the world would appear to the child whose worldview of basic trust in his or her primary adult relationships was blocked or failed to develop. Imagine how a newborn baby feels being separated from his or her mother at birth. Suddenly they find themselves in a strange new world. The familiar sounds, smells, feelings, reassurance of mom's warmth and heartbeat, bond of basic trust, and reassuring reference to interpret new experiences are gone. Babies must face what may appear to be the nightmare of birth alone. Do they relax, embrace and play with each new sight, sound, or texture? No. They curl into a tight ball and defend themselves against an unknown and frightening world. Separation anxiety and feelings of abandonment are considered the greatest threats to the infant or early child. Imagine the confusion an infant feels being placed in a day-care facility, attended by different caretakers. The consistent reference the child needs to interpret the world, to give it order and meaning, is gone. Basic trust is replaced by uncertainty. When we break the learning channel we call bonding, development is compromised on every level.

Is bonding really all that important? The terrorist attack on the World Trade Center, September 11th 2001, was a grim reminder that the twentieth century was a century of World Wars, unparalleled in human history. Little progress has been made in preventing personal and global violence. James W. Prescott's theoretical and scientific research on the developmental origins of love and violence cuts to the core of our personal and global violence. The closer we come to the source of our pain, however, the more we tend to defend against it, a response that often blinds us to the obvious.

Human love begins *in utero,* is carried through pregnancy, birth

Once a culture or person collapses into anxiety, no self-effort is effective against that negative power. Only insight has the power to override that negativity and bring the system into balance. Operation bootstrap always fails. Wholeness of mind can't come from any action or thought from a split person, but only through a kind of grace, the power of insight arriving full-blown into the brain.
Bond of Power

and the postnatal nurturance of bonding and breast-feeding. Yet, the most critical, formative relationship—one that encodes the developing brain for a lifetime of affection or rage—the relationship between mother and infant, is not valued, nurtured or supported by our culture. Infants and young children are often not held, touched, or played with. The majority of babies are placed in institutionalized childcare. Television and computers have replaced imaginative play between adults and children. Failing the early bond, which is intimately linked to direct and sustained physical contact between mother and infant, the future of later love relationships are threatened, as is society itself. Unbonded behaviors result in an alienated, aggressive emotional/social/sexual cycle that affects mother, baby, family, society and now, the world.

As the health scientist administrator of the developmental behavioral biology program at the National Institute of Child Health and Human Development (1966-1980), James W. Prescott established research programs which documented that failed mother love in primates result in developmental brain disorders that lead to lifelong patterns of depression, violence and drug addiction. His research, and that of many others, leaves little doubt that nothing can replace the loving touch, breast-feeding, and emotional nurturing shared by mother and infant.

> Violence involves two fundamental issues. One is the bonded and unbonded child. The other is full gender equality. Until women are able to control their own body, and not just reproduction, but the whole spectrum of their sexuality, it will be very difficult to achieve the first step, which is the bonded child. Look at all the violence against women, the rapes, domestic violence, battered women, it's epidemic, as is child abuse and neglect. What causes the anger and rage which leads to this violence? The ability to experience joy and pleasure.

> With the basic trust that affectionate pleasure develops we respond more openly to life and to change. People who are rigid, highly armored, are limited in their capacity to feel empathy, compassion or adapt to change, which translates into a lack of bonding and limited capacity to nurture others.

> We have a moral philosophy which says that pleasure and the body

Maria Montessori claimed that a humankind abandoned in its early formative period becomes the worst threat to its own survival. Allen Schore's research shows that a form of semi-abandonment happens to all of us, perpetuates our culture, and seriously impairs our emotional-relational system itself.
The Biology of Transcendence

is evil and the spirit or soul is good. There is a division between the natural state of the body and our ideas about good and evil. We are at war with our own bodies and in many ways women, their bodies and children are the targets in this war. This repression of pleasure sets up the reservoir of rage; and our belief systems create the target. Both work together. We have to look at sexuality quite differently, that is, as an integral part of who we are.

The child, roughing in a world of knowledge, wanders without rhyme or reason, and s/he plays. S/he has no goals other than the moment, and no other time exists. To the child the time is always now, the place always here, the center is always "me."
Magical Child

Children are punished for touching their genitals which creates a neural-dissociative state in the brain. The sensory deprivation of pleasure results in the failure of certain neural pathways to properly develop. Sensory stimulation acts like a nutrient for brain growth and development. The richer the networks, the greater the interconnectivity and neural integration of the brain. If we do not get the sensory stimulation we equate with love, bonding and intimacy during the formative periods of brain development, we will be impaired, if not crippled in our ability to experience and express this "language of love" later in life.

Giving and receiving pleasure releases oxytocin, a hormone associated with love and bonding. The pleasure associated with placing the newborn at the breast of the mother at birth, and maintaining close physical body contact reestablishes the prenatal bond. The medical profession routinely separates the baby from the mother.

In the late '50s and '60s Harry Harlow separated infant monkeys from their mothers and housed them alone in cages. These infants protested by crying and extreme agitation. When the bond was not reestablished, the infant monkeys became profoundly depressed, engaged in chronic rocking behaviors, self-stimulation, and tactile avoidance.

By depriving intimate body contact between mother and infant, the sensory systems needed to experience pleasure, bonding and love were starved. Harlow created emotionally, socially and sexually dysfunctional animals. They became pathological as juveniles and adults. Their reproductive systems were intact, but the emotional and social skills we associate with love and bonding were destroyed.

No mammal, except the human mammal separates the newborn

from its mother. Rare, historical footage of this pioneering research along with current research on bonding and early brain development is now available at www://TTFuture.org.

Bonding creates the sensory and emotional environment that shapes how we interpret and respond to relationships life long. Break the bond at the beginning and we set the stage for cycles of depression, anger, rage, substance abuse and violence, generation after generation.

Personal Interview
James W. Prescott, Ph.D.
Brain & Behavior Neuroscientist, Anthropologist

Primary Learning & Conditioning

In the 1970s the Carnegie Foundation did a study on learning and retention. They found that as much as 95 percent of all learning is *primary*. By primary we mean the learning that occurs spontaneously through encountering, embracing, and playing with our environment. In terms of brain growth and development, more is learned in the first year of life than all the years that follow. Learning to walk and talk, perhaps two of the most challenging tasks we will ever undertake, unfolds spontaneously in our first eighteen months, with little or no coaching. Primary learning occurs naturally.

As toddlers, for example, we observed mom open and close a cupboard door. Without coaching or rewards, we scoot over and pull on the handle. We pull again and again, harder and harder. Suddenly the door flies open and down we go. Up we crawl to do it again, and again, with this door and all the other doors we can find. Soon we discover that trash cans have lids that open and close, open and close. The same is true of toilet seats and jewelry boxes. Lids here, lids there, hundreds of lids, thousands of lids, millions and billions and trillions of lids. And all because we saw mama open a cupboard door. Mom modeled a possibility. She represented the *model imperative*, and our life was transformed.

The vast majority of learning is primary. We are completely *in* the experience. There is no *me* standing aside, witnessing, judging, praising, or criticizing. All of our available energy and attention is given to this new expanding relationship. There is no time, no conflict. The relationship is play. Play is learning. We are the Zone!

Anxiety is always the enemy of intelligence and always blocks the biological plan. The minute anxiety arises, intelligence closes to a search for anything that will relive the anxiety. This might lead to a street-smart mentality or to precocity along narrow culturally approved lines, but the biological plan will have been aborted.
Magical Child

Suddenly there is a tremor in the force. The phone rings and mama's dinner guests will arrive in thirty minutes. Her relationship to *her* world has changed and so has ours. The free, open, yet incomplete exploration of hinges and doors is no longer safe. Why? Because mama just told us to stop! At that moment our complete attention split between learning and avoiding conflict with mama. The safe place she represented suddenly became a threat.

We continue our playful banging on the cupboard door, but now with one eye on mama. She places three red paper cups on the floor, to distract us, and smiles. We're not convinced. (Bruno Bettleheim claimed that adults cannot lie to a child. Regardless what adults say, children are participating in the adult field, reading it, learning from it.) We sense her attempt to divert our attention.

The pot mama is stirring boils over and so does she. Tension builds. Our attention now splits again between mama, the stupid paper cups, and those enchanting hinges. We bang the door again, and then again. Mama stomps her foot and yells. As our split attention and conflict increase we experience a corresponding decrease in learning, performance, and well-being. Learning is relationship and relationships are state specific.

Primary learning is free from conflict. We call it play. With primary learning, or play, the activity itself is so rewarding that we disappear into it. Thought, feeling, and action are completely focused on this new learning relationship, right now. It is only when danger or conflict arises that part of our attention is diverted for defense. Only then is there a separate self-image, or "me," witnessing, watching, and protecting itself. The greater the need for protection, the less attention there is to meet the challenge and learn.

> When I play the identity I know as Fred disappears. Only to the extent that the social categories disappear can play happen. Real play begins with the disappearance of that social/cultural image we have about ourselves.
>
> Personal Interview
> ## O. Fred Donaldson, Ph.D.
> Author, *Playing by Heart*

When a line forms between child play and adult work, the interaction between human and earth collapses. We are then isolated with our own energies, and work we must, indeed. The problem set for us is not to try to turn back to aboriginal man: that is impossible. The problem, if we are to survive, is to erase the line between work and play. Only then is personal power amplified... With a technological human, the resulting power would be awesome and magnificent indeed, were s/he in a balanced bonding with the earth, and that may be the direction toward which the world is tending.
Magical Child

Play, Practice & Work

The bell rings. School is out. We are free, finally free. To what? To mess around, sleep in, dream, tear apart grandpa's radio, catch tadpoles and watch-em grow legs, build forts, dig tunnels to China, dress up like a princess, sneak a peak at dad's Playboy magazine, make pudding, jump on a pogo-stick 10,001 times. Now that the important stuff we call work is done, we can play. By implication, work and school are important, fun and play are not. To most, the word *play* means not-serious, unimportant, frivolous. Or play means an activity, such as "playing ball" or "playing a violin," which most often really means practice. To play with a violin is very different from practicing with a violin.

The words "working hard" conjure images of tense muscles, concentration, and strained faces. Playing hard may involve all these qualities, but the image is somehow different—softer, less tense or constrained. Working implies that we are accomplishing some goal, that we are "making something of ourselves." Playing implies we are wasting valuable time, time that many adults feel should be put to better use by working. The older children get, the less time they can "waste" playing. For most, growing up means transforming playtime into work time. It's a jungle out there; survival of the fittest. Or is it?

Intelligence, like the body, can be injured or nurtured, stimulated or starved.
Magical Child

> All the people who "get there" get there because they love what they are doing. They're not driven by a work ethic; they're driven by a love ethic. Michael Jordan plays very hard, very indulgently. Ben Hogan hit tens of thousands of balls because he loved to hit golf balls. That gets mistaken by the intellect as work. "If you work hard enough, son, and if you keep your nose to the grindstone, son, then you will be able to perform like these people." This is absolutely not the case, not true. The great performers perform as they do, and do so with such ease, because they love what they are doing. It's not work. It's play.
>
> Personal Interview
> ## Chuck Hogan
> Author, Educator, Performance Specialist

We get the message very early: play will be tolerated as long as we have done a good job "working hard." Have you ever heard, at a school or during a corporate awards ceremony, "We'd like to recognize Mary Jones. Mary, please step up here. You've been awarded the blue ribbon, a certificate of excellence for messing around"?

Remember that play really means to adults something that is not serious. It's the time left over. The problem is that very early on, those activities that we loved to do just because it was so much fun, also become encompassed by the cultural idea of competition. Then, for adults and increasingly for children, play becomes as serious as going to law school, doing mathematics, and competing for a job.

Personal Interview
O. Fred Donaldson, Ph.D.
Author *Playing by Heart*

Play Ages & Stages

What we play "with" changes at different ages and stages of development. The state of original play remains the same. Newborns play with nipples. The early child plays with trucks and sand. Teens play with clothes. Michael Jordan plays with basketballs. Physicists play with ideas. If optimum learning, performance, and wellness are our goals, we will maintain this playful relationship as new capacities unfold.

Neuroscientist Paul MacLean spoke of three lifelong, indispensable requirements we have, expressed from the moment of birth. He called this the family triad of needs, needs that are primary and interdependent; each gives rise to and supports the other. They are *audiovisual communication, nurturing,* and *play.*

Every stage of development is complete and perfect within itself. The three-year-old is not an incomplete five-year-old; the child is not an incomplete adult. Never are we simply on our way; always, we have arrived.
Magical Child

Play, like audiovisual communication and nurturing, changes as the infant-child grows; a process marked by distinct stages. Almost as clearly defined as the rings of a tree, a child's growth unfolds in the natural, evolutionary order nature followed in the long history of our species' development. A sensory-motor brain unfolds first, then our emotional-cognitive system, then the several sections of the *neocortex,* or new brain. Each brings a new and expanded form of play as it unfolds, and a full unfolding depends on that play.

Play marks the development and use of each of these neural systems, and so grows more complex, rich, diversified, and rewarding as it expands in response to each new neural unfolding. The more expansive and rich the neural structure, the more expansive and rich the intelligence and play that both result from and bring about such growth.

The brain is "experience-dependent," as Allan Schore calls it, which means the actual growth of individual brain cells and their linkage-expansion into "structures of knowledge" depend on corresponding interactions with and responses from the environment. The earliest environment, and the most permanently influential, is the mother.

Smiles

A newborn infant will smile when we speak to it close up, say six to twelve inches away. This is audiovisual communication and a first play with the infant. Peek-a-boo soon follows: when face appears, infant's smile breaks out; face disappears, smile fades; reappears, smiles. Two or three repetitions and infant catches on that play is taking place, expects the face to disappear and reappear and soon laughs delightedly at each. The words "peek-a-boo" are an integral part of the action, adding that auditory aspect; all of this is learning, and learning is play.

Soon the infant initiates peek-a-boo, as while nursing; the infant finds that it can bring about the play, disappearing behind the breast, appearing, finding those eyes talking back, disappearing again, over and over. Delighted. Playing with the nipple, a game of loss-recovery, is a form of peek-a-boo. Associative learning unfolds in this way. New neural links form in all these varieties of play.

Nearly any repeated audiovisual action signals play, invites imitation. The newborn will stick out its tongue when we stick out ours. The mirroring between model and child begins at the beginning. Interaction is a two-way street. Infant finds that one can initiate and elicit response from out-there, as well as receive from and respond to that-out-there. *Play gives dominion over one's world.*

Baubles hung over a crib catch infant's eye, but this is not audiovisual communication. It is a form of entertainment, better than a blank wall perhaps, but a poor excuse for that face and all that goes with it. Far better than crib and bangle-dangling is the snugli for "baby wearing." And not the outward-facing child carrier, which offers no face for communication and gives the infant a feeling of constant falling forward. The snugli with that magical face and heart six to twelve inches away, works best by far. Communication involves eyes and voice, a voice to which infant has responded since the fifth month in utero.

To shift from the womb, or from any matrix, is to be "born out of it" and into another one. The nature of our growth is such that each matrix is larger and less constricting, or more abstract and less concrete than the previous one. Each matrix encompasses more possibility and power, and should provide an increasingly safer place to stand. At each matrix-shift, the brain undergoes a growth spurt, which prepares it for massive and rapid new learning. The mind/brain learns by exploring the new matrix and construction a conceptual pattern of it, which means a sensory integration of that matrix; a structure of knowledge of it as Piaget would say or a "mathematical inter-weaving of energies," as Bohm might say.
Bond of Power

High Chair Play

All children in all cultures will turn every event into play when allowed; thus, every event can be an occasion for learning, if allowed. At the highchair stage, feeding is prime-time play. A bite rejected and spit out, offered again, is rejected again. Twice is repetition; any repetitive action is an invitation to play. Infant knocks or throws its spoon on the floor, caretaker picks it up. Infant does it again, caretaker retrieves. Soon infant is in near hysterics with laughter, throwing the spoon with greater and greater abandon and excitement. A ball rolled across table toward infant invites the attempt to return and is a source of endless delight. New visual and motor skills expand with each playful encounter of this sort.

The infant is delighted when learning, since that is what the brain is designed to do. But the action offered must fit the age and stage. Just as we wouldn't feed steak and champagne to the newborn, nor Pablum to the adolescent, we don't feed later forms of play to the early child. I see no advantage to flash cards and alphabet-number learning in the crib or even early years. There are too many stage-appropriate needs crying to be met. Why not meet them instead of spending this age trying to prepare for what you think might be the needs for the next stage? Take your cues from your child and your child will take its cues from you. If little else is offered, infant-children may respond to flash cards, even with the pleased expression at your approval, but not with that ecstatic enthusiasm of play.

Toddlers

In the toddler period the possibilities of play expand exponentially. Up on those hind legs charging about to explore every nook and cranny, building new neural structures of knowledge through taste, touch, smell, seeing, and hearing. All is pure play and playful learning.

"No!" and "Don't!" suppress learning, play, and joy, while bringing a release of cortisol, a depressant in that toddler's body and brain. There is no learning in a state of depression, though there is a kind of animal conditioning. Play is a high-cortical, or new-brain, response, and the negative state generated by "No" and "Don't" brings an ancient, sensory-motor "hindbrain" reaction of defense. A child grows by encouragement and support, not by negative restraint. "No" and "Don't" are toxic.

Sitting on the floor rolling the ball back and forth with a caretaker is endless delight to the toddler. The activity builds spatial intelligence, motor coordination, and an open, trusting responsiveness to the environment and caretaker. Singing-movement games, as used by Education Through Music (ETM), are perfect for toddlers.

The three or four-year-old child can spend endless hours alone, looking into a mud puddle or pool, watching the most minute creatures and forms of life. Children need great open spaces of time in which to do nothing apparent to an onlooker. The world is brand new throughout childhood.

Storytelling

Storytelling is a joy to a child, and storytelling and play are intertwined and mutually reinforcing. Young children go catatonic during storytelling; jaws drop down, eyes stare at the storyteller, bodies are motionless. They are not seeing the storytellers but watching the unfolding inner world storytelling brings about. The brain automatically creates inner worlds of imagery in response to those magical words of a story, a construction job employing every aspect of brain and body. Building inner worlds of imagery expands the neural fields, links structures of knowledge, and builds new structures.

Children want to hear the same story over and over, just as they want peek-a-boo or "catch" repeated endlessly. Repetition stabilizes the new neural links brought about in such activities. (This is called *myelination*.) At a certain point the child will act those inner story pictures out in imaginative play, projecting their inner image on some outer object. Having heard the tale of *The Three Bears* over and over, toddler finds a collection of empty bottles and selects a big, middle-sized, and small one that become Papa, Mamma, and Baby Bear. *The Three Bears* is enacted through these three symbolic figures, over and over. When one object stands for another object in this fashion, metaphoric and/or symbolic action takes place. Metaphor and symbol are the foundations of all great intellectual ventures later in life. All alphabets, numerals, and written signs are metaphoric or symbolic.

Monkey See - Monkey Do

Imitative play fills the early years. The two-year-old sees mother making cookies and follows suit. A jar top becomes the mixing bowl, a stick the spoon, some dirt or mud the dough. Seeing the great bowl in the jar top, spoon in the stick, is metaphoric thinking, transferring information from one category of being to another. Michelangelo sees the figure in the stone before he picks up his chisel.

No!, and eventually any relative negative, triggers up flight-fight arousals of saber-tooth origin, translating through our ancient amygdala. An emphatic harsh NO! and our poor dog curls up, tail between legs, a look of crushed sadness, shame, and guilt on her face, begging for forgiveness. Our animal brains are shared systems and never forget.
[*The amygdala, recall, is a critical neural module involved in memory, particularly flight-fight decisions, and a kind of halfway house communicating between reptilian and mammalian brains. Virtually all memories of the first three years involve the amygdala.]*

The Biology of Transcendence

Our four-year-old sees a mighty road roller rumbling down the street and wants to take part in such tremendous action. He finds a spool in mother's cabinet and it becomes the mighty road roller. His inner image of that great machine to which he has no access, over which he has no control, is projected on this tiny object over which he does have access and control, and for hours he plays in a "modulated world" of his own making, a perfect example of metaphoric-symbolic action. To "see" or interpret one form or meaning from another is a high-level, abstract form of thinking.

This leads, years later, to being able to look at a mathematical, algebraic or chemical equation and "see" what it implies—the possibilities it holds—and forms the basis of a love for playing with such adult toys. The foundation of the latter complexity is based squarely on the former simplicity. The child who never plays will not be able to play, neither with music nor mathematics and its theorems, nor architectural designs nor the great philosophies of life.

Child of the Dream

The four- to seven-year-old is "a child of the dream" as Piaget put it, living in a dream world of her own creation, occasionally playing her dreams out on the stage of the world-out-there shared with parent and others. The daydreaming child is laying the foundation for great thoughts later on. Years ago Harvard's Burton White found that the one shared characteristic of all brilliant and happy children was that they spent long hours in open-eyed, blank staring.

Group play, unless under the guidance of an adult and handled with great understanding, empathy, insight, and care, as in Education Through Music (ETM), has little meaning to the early child. Play is either solitary or with the parent, by and large. At around age five or so a contemporary may be sought out to engage in imaginative play, where each child pretends they are some imagined character. The majority of time, however, five-year-olds play in their private worlds, projecting in them the presence of the other. Seldom do they actually join in what adults think of as organized games unless strongly encouraged to do so by adults.

Play-Talk

Virtually all play in the early years involves verbal play. The child talks his play, plays out his world through speech. Alexandria Luria traced the

Our children do mirror us, as they must, as we mirrored our parents, and had to. Each next generation proves anxiety-ridden, half-mad, antisocial, depressed idiots, drowning themselves in alcohol and "disappointing" our hopes that this time it might be different. By our fruits, we should recognize our state. We reap as we sow and as was sowed for us. Mind-in-here mirrors world-out-there, we become as we behold.
Bond of Power

profound relationships between sensory-motor development, language, and learning in general, all coordinating in play. As children talk out their world experience of play, they furnish their own magical Word, which is given through storytelling. They act out their own inner stories through outer speech and actions. This pattern of hearing Word and making a muscular response to it begins in utero.

Social needs may enter around age seven, at the earliest, and that need is most comfortably met by one other child, maybe two at most. (Even among three children two will probably pair off. The human wasn't made for large numbers, not even in the late period of childhood. Six or seven is a crowd. "All the boys are going out," the seven or eight-year-old announces. All half-dozen or so.) Group play is not competitive during this middle child period. Competition kills this play. Winning or losing have no place at this stage. No learning takes place from winning or losing. The musical games of Education Through Music (ETM) are perfect for both the early and middle child and offer all the social interaction needed.

Three's a Crowd

Two or three children of the middle period will gather and play "let's pretend" for hours. This consists of one scenario after another being presented orally by each child. No one carries through on any single item of pretense, each but spins off from the other on another "let's pretend" of her own making. This oral play can go on for hours, particularly among girls. Little boys tend more toward acting out their spoken play.

Middle children (approximately ages seven to puberty) live out and become their own metaphors. Leaping through the branches, the boys will act out Tarzan and the apes, or cowboys and Indians, following their own verbal cues. "Play like we're Luke Skywalker" or whoever the current hero figure might be. The spindly little tike becomes the mighty space-hero in his own mind's eye. No longer are all projections made onto outer objects; one's own body becomes the target of the inner image, granting might and dominion over the child world.

Children "come down into their body" at age seven, as Rudolph Steiner expressed it. The left hemisphere takes over from the dreaming right, and control and mastery of this newly discovered body becomes sheer joy. The boy wants to climb every tree, leap every obstacle, run like the wind. The little girl will jump rope endlessly, past all count. Play and development are

Two categories of play are observed in the child according to Piaget: fantasy play and imitative play. Both forms use imagination, which is defined as "creating an image not present to the senses."… In fantasy play, the child registers stimuli from part of his/her world… and makes the object serve his/her fantasy image by transforming it to match that fantasy image, and his/her play is with that transformed object. The child has, at this point, bent the world to the service of desire… In imitative play, the child acts as though s/he is the adult model s/he is imitating, and the purpose of the imitations is to assume the powers of the adult imitated… Imitation serves the same function as fantasy play …The central act of mind in both cases is imagination.
Magical Child

intertwined at every stage. Coming into full awareness of body is a major event and calls for near-constant movement. School desks are a disaster at this point.

Rough and Tumble

During preschool and elementary school years, on playgrounds all over the world, children, "when allowed," particularly boys, engage repetitively and very vigorously in what looks like aggressive mayhem; teasing, hitting, pushing, pouncing, chasing, poking, sneaking up on, piling on, games with changeable rules, and general play fighting are the norm. A closer look reveals not aggressive mayhem, but a particular variety of behavior known as *rough and tumble play.*

The most fascinating experiences for the child are nearly always those of the parents: the mysteries of cooking and kitchen gadgetry, the tools for making and repairing an automobile engine or a sewing machine. S/he will explore according to the nature of his/her own exploratory tools, the five senses. Through physical encounters with the tangible world of things, the mind-brain structures its corresponding knowledge of that world. The parents do not try to engineer this learning because they know that learning is a nonconscious process that must simply be allowed to unfold.

Magical Child

The participants are usually smiling, whooping, and, from their viewpoint are having a great time. They know they are playing. Dominance is not the primary issue, but toughness is. Rough and tumble play is a special play activity that helps to develop strong and flexible affiliations and friendships. When a bully or a controlling adult takes over, the play changes its character, losing its free-ranging nature.

With adolescence rough and tumble play is gradually replaced. The activity becomes more competitive and acquires dominance-power qualities, with winning and losing replacing the spontaneous give and take seen in earlier times. Experiencing this special play activity in the early years seems to be important. Missing it seems to produce unwanted consequences.

In a comparison-control study of 36 adult homicidal males, anecdotal playground and family reports revealed a near absence of give and take playground anarchy. The "normal" and nonviolent comparison control group provided descriptions of give and take, winning and losing in playground games, and often remembered the names and characteristics of buddies with whom they had rough-and-tumbled experiences. None of the violent males remembered a playground buddy. Play histories of 8000 psychiatric outpatients seem to support the conclusion that rough and tumble play prepares those who successfully enjoyed it for a more flexible, socially competent future.

Similar play behavior is seen in the wild. When an adult Silverback gorilla, for example, enters the play-space, it is usually to break up a real fight that began as rough and tumble play. When juvenile primates sense danger or that no adult is "on call" to break up a serious situation the play also ceases. For primates and for human beings, an adult in the wings, but not on scene creates the "safe place" for this high-energy play to unfold.

When our children whoop it up in rough and tumble activities, most adults become uncomfortable. Their discomfort and need to take "responsible control" usually ends the free play for kids. Surveys of young adult female teachers show their general anxiety in the presence of, and lack of accurate "knowledge about," this important developmental play-behavior. Adult "organized" play activities, including sports, does not replace the freedom and exuberance or provide the developmental rewards gained from open, adult-at-a-distance rough and tumble play. Rough and tumble play is important to children and it is important that adults understand and create the safe place for this free-range, vigorous activity.

Personal Play Interview
Stuart Brown, M.D.
Author, PBS Producer

Fred Donaldson observes that rough and tumble play is often viewed and understood from within the cultural framework that play is a contest. Contests seem so normal and natural, after all, "boys will be boys."

From the very beginning children know this activity is deceitfully serious. There are winners and losers. And the consequences escalate. From cultural view of play, this is how we teach males to be contestants; how to "play the game."

On the other hand, there is something that I call play that looks like the same thing but is fundamentally different. There are different roles, different patterns of movement, different relationships, and different outcomes. Play and contests may look the same but they have very different intentions. The meaning of the activity, what is learned is completely different. There is no failure possible in original play. Contests have winners and losers. It is not the activity, rather the nature and quality of the relationship to the activity that determine if the rough and tumble is play or not.

Personal Interview
O. Fred Donaldson, Ph.D.
Play Explorer, Author: _Playing By Heart_

With an infinitely open neural capacity, seven- to eleven-year-old children have no limitations and consider all possibilities equally valid. The only qualification is nature's imperative that they be given appropriate cultural models and environment. Ernest Hilgard points out that this middle child becomes acutely sensitive to suggestions concerning personal possibility. This susceptibility to suggestion peaks around age eleven and closes by about age fourteen in most of us. The subtle suggestions, implications, even hazy ideas held by parents, peers, or superiors concerning who we are and what our possibilities are or aren't profoundly impact children. They pick up our inherent beliefs and social notions whether expressed or not, and automatically reflect them. Their limitless possibilities for new patterns of conception and perception will be limited by the nature of their models, with no one the wiser.

Evolution's End

Groupies

Group games enter at around age ten or eleven, if a group is available. Neighborhood "pick-up" games have all but disappeared. In the past these group games were not competitive in a win-lose sense. "Giant-steps, baby-steps" gave way to "Red Rover come over," hide and seek, capture the flag… the list of group games were endless. These self-organized activities laid the foundation for social skills, give and take, fairness, and consideration for the other, but such noble issues are never in the mind of the playing child, nor can they be taught or talked about. The child finds out about them through group play.

Board games also come with the later years of the middle child, around age ten or eleven. Monopoly can be a fascination, for instance, though this involves winning-losing and is border line, appealing to the border line pre-puberty child. Children will seek out their own level, find ways to fill their own needs.

Group ball games enter with the pre-puberty child, but winning or losing is not part of the picture as yet. Sides are chosen for fairness, so to speak, equal weight and ability. Each side gets its share of strong and weak, husky and skinny. The sheer joy of throwing the ball, connecting with the bat, the dash for first base, snagging a ball out of thin air against all odds, those are the rewards—and they are monumental.

"All they want to do is play." A child's relentless absorption in play seems to be a problem for adults... His/her intent is to play with the world; whereas our intentions are to make him or her attend to our ideas of work.
Magical Child

Whose side wins or loses is beside the point. No one keeps score in this middle-year ball game since each plays for his own expression, his or her own delight, and sides change continually as a game goes along. New players arrive, having finished some home chore, and others may be called home, the sides shifting to maintain balance.

Arguments over tipping the ball for a foul, tagging a runner at second in time, catching the ball fair before falling, can become heated and passionate, occupying half the play time, and are a critical part of the play. The social learning of give and take is immense in this. Democracy is in action.

No Grown-ups Allowed!

Adults with their rules, regulations and decision-making, kill all this. The child loses his or her own world in becoming the object of a spectator. Each plays for his own joy, not someone else's entertainment. Play disappears in the presence of adults; judgment enters. Face-saving becomes an issue, disgrace a possibility. On their own, the later middle child is self-governing and, above all, fair. Fairness disappears when adults call the shots. Little League has been a major disaster to American childhood. More about this when we look more closely at athletics and the intelligence of play.

With puberty the "herd instinct" of the gene pool enters the scene, and play reflects it. Competition may enter the scene with pre-adolescence, and winning can become critical. Then it becomes more important than ever that these late-childhood participants work out their own salvation in their games. If adults interfere with their judgments and supervision, most of this social learning is lost. The "coach" is, with rare exceptions, a disaster when it comes to developing the social skills this play should build. These young people don't need coaching, they need to discover self-monitoring and how to achieve group consensus on their own; they need to learn how to take their lumps on occasion and still belong to the play group; to give over some element of personal freedom or judgment on behalf of the larger good. The presence of adults, or worse still, the coaching of adults, alters the meaning of the experience dramatically.

Young people will naturally and spontaneously develop these skills if left alone, but not completely alone. An adult in the wings, but not on scene, creates the "safe place" for this high-energy play to unfold. When the adult enters the play space, as a dominant parent or coach, this self-regulated play-learning disappears. If we want children to be self-sufficient parts of a self-ruling democracy we won't interfere. Remember Stuart Brown's description of the Silverback. Wild animals play freely unless a predator or human comes on the scene, at which point play disappears and alert defensiveness takes its place. Our children are no different.

Do It Yourself!

Entertainment is not play and play *is* learning. Certain limited forms of information might be exchanged through entertainment, but this is not learning in the sense considered here. Watching a ball game is a counterfeit experience that may be peculiarly frustrating; the spectator's lack of personal involvement may build toward suppressed rage. Some sports arenas and coliseums have become tinderboxes ready to explode. Spending time together is nice but taking your son or daughter to the ball game, an entertainment, a spectator event that may last virtually all day, isn't half worth five minutes of tossing a ball with that child. Think of what is

Intelligence is the ability to interact, and the ability to interact has not increased through technology. It has decreased. We have long spoken of our technological devices as "extensions" of our personal power; telescopes, microscopes, and so on extending our vision; telephones and radios our hearing... and so on. In practice, though, every technological achievement undermines, erodes, even replaces, in one way or another, our ability it "extends and enhances." Instead of extending and increasing personal power, our devices sharply reduce it.

Any reduction in personal power produces anxiety, as millions of years of genetic encoding and expectancies begin to be shortchanged. The paradox is that our anxiety has increased proportionately, (in fact widely out of proportion) with our technological "advances" which should, by all rights, reduce anxiety.
Bond of Power

involved—running, catching, laughing, tumbling in the grass; the whole body, all the senses are involved. Compare this, in terms of whole body engagement, use and development, to sitting in the stands all day. The more sensory involvement, the greater the growth and development.

Television & Computer Play

For years computer companies and users have been touting the "whole brain" and "complex" thinking abilities developed by computer games, most often to offset the violent and aggressive content of most popular games. Tracy McVeigh, education editor of the British publication *The Observer*, reviewed disturbing research on computer use, brain development, and aggression.

All this indicates a biocultural effect, wherein our biology influences our culture and our culture influences our biology. A sufficient number of children born predisposed toward defensiveness and quick reflexive survival reactions will tend to change the nature of the society in which they grow up.... Angry defensive people tend to clone their condition in the next generation, civilized society disappears and culture is born, growing more and more explosive and dangerous with each generation.

The Biology of Transcendence

> Computer games are creating a dumbed-down generation of children far more disposed to violence than their parents, according to a controversial new study. The tendency to lose control is not due to children absorbing the aggression involved in the computer game itself, as previous researchers have suggested, but rather to the damage done by stunting the developing mind.

> Using the most sophisticated technology available, the level of brain activity was measured in hundreds of teenagers playing a Nintendo game and compared to the brain scans of other students doing a simple, repetitive arithmetical exercise. To the surprise of brain-mapping expert Professor Ryuta Kawashima and his team at Tohoku University in Japan, it was found that the computer game only stimulated activity in the parts of the brain associated with vision and movement. In contrast, arithmetic stimulated brain activity in both the left and right hemispheres of the frontal lobe - the area of the brain most associated with learning, memory and emotion.

> Most worrying of all was that the frontal lobe, which continues to develop in humans until the age of about 20, also has an important role to play in keeping an individual's behavior in check. Children often do things they shouldn't because their frontal lobes are underdeveloped. The more work done to thicken the fibers connecting the neurons in this part of the brain, the better the child's ability will be to control their behavior. The more this area is stimulated, the more these fibers will thicken. The students who played computer games were halting the process of brain development and affecting their ability to control potentially anti-social elements of their behavior.

The Optimum Learning Relationship

The implications are very serious for an increasingly violent society. Kawashima says the message to parents was clear. "Children need to be encouraged to learn basic reading and writing, of course," he said. "But the other thing is to ask them to play outside with other children and interact and to communicate with others as much as possible."

The Observer, August 19, 2001

Marshall McLuhan noted years ago, "The medium *is* the message." It is the machine, not the program content that determines what regions of the brain are used while interacting with that technology, be it a drill press, computer, or a television screen. The brain responds to a given technology with essentially the same "neuro-pattern" each time the technology is encountered. Program content has virtually no impact on brain growth and development, especially during the most sensitive periods of development.

In the first encounter, which involves play, the child learns how to interact with a television screen. The play lasts a few minutes, just long enough to develop a "relationship" with an unknown object. This new and unknown relationship demands complete attention, a basic characteristic of play. Once the relationship is developed, with its corresponding brain growth, play stops and is replaced by entertainment. Entertainment requires very little attention compared to the total entrainment found in play. The relationship to television, and corresponding brain growth created in the first encounter, is then reused with each subsequent encounter with that device. In terms of brain growth and development, each of the 5,000 hours the average child devotes to television viewing by age five might as well have been a rerun of the original program. This is *the* critical point, in terms of brain growth, up to and including age ten or eleven. As we described earlier, entertainment is not learning.

Play can be completely entertaining. Entertainment is not play, however. And don't forget, computers, televisions, and video technologies are "imaging" systems. They display counterfeits of the internal images naturally produced by the brain. As described earlier, images are the basic operating system of the brain. The brain communicates its life and death information through images. Counterfeit images easily deceive the emotional, cognitive, and sensory motor regions of the brain. These older and more primary centers can not distinguish between the natural images produced by the brain and its counterfeit. These brain centers simply respond to a given

Television replaced storytelling in most homes, and it changed the radio from a storyteller to a music box... Television also replaced family conversation in general...With television on the scene, parents rarely played with children. All sat around the box, and even playing among siblings disappeared. Thus no capacity for play and its internal imaging developed. Nintendo does not and cannot replace imaginative play.
Evolution's End

stimulus, in this case the image, and stimulus *is* real. The images on the movie screen are real images. The sounds amplified by multimillion-dollar Dolby and THX technologies are real sounds.

The technologies for creating and displaying moving pictures are less than a century old, a nanosecond in biological time. Charlie Chaplin is a mere blink on the counterfeit Richter scale compared to the images now being mass-produced by today's graphic animation technologies. The more realistic, intense and evocative the counterfeit, the stronger the response of our two primary brain centers. This explains why we scream, cry and are so easily aroused by the images displayed on film, television and computers. The effect of these images is immediate. The seeing is the effect. What we "think" about these images occurs much later, way down the synaptic stream. Millions of emotional and physical connections cascade through the entire body before we are even aware that we have seen the image. The people who create these devices and their images know this. Deception is their craft. And we love being deceived. But at what price? We will deal more with computers and television in part two when we explore the role of imagination in Optimum Learning Relationships.

Television floods the brain with a counterfeit of the response the brain is supposed to learn to make to the stimuli of words or music. As a result, much of the structural coupling between mind and environment is eliminated; few metaphoric images develop; few higher cortical areas of the brain are called into play; few, if any, symbolic structures develop. E=MC² will be just marks on paper, for there will be no metaphoric ability to transfer those symbols to the neocortex for conceptualization, and subsequently, no development of its main purpose; symbolic conceptual systems.
Evolution's End

The Art of Play

Art is the high point of play from the earliest child period throughout life. From the crude stick-drawings of the four-year-old to the most advanced form of painting or design, from the first singing-stories of ETM to playing Beethoven's *Apassionata,* from sand castle at the beach to Michelangelo's *David*, art is play, and those who can play fully are always the ones most happy in any form of art, and who turn any activity into art, whether it be politics, education, finance, science, or what-have-you. Any form of play is a form of art and vice-versa. When anthropologist Margaret Mead said that only an education founded on art will ever succeed, she meant that all subjects must be presented as an art form. Learning must be an esthetic experience, appreciated and enjoyed. William Blake's statement that mechanical excellence is the vehicle of genius, simply means the neural structures must be there, practiced until fully in place, for the highest form of creativity to manifest. And one builds those structures from the beginning through play. As clearly depicted in Waldorf Education, "the art of living and learning" begins very early in life. If we learn of life through play, we will play through life as an artist, regardless of the road taken. Which means also that we would play to the very end of life.

Adult Play

Adult play can embrace all forms of play leading up to it and opens to a field of play without boundaries. The challenge for adults is that many have been adulterated, play deprived. Cultural models of contest and competition replaced their original play state very early. Only one can win. All the rest are losers. We politely say, it is how we play the game that counts, but everyone knows the truth. The goal is to win.

> It goes back to this issue of being safe enough to play the game freely. If you're not safe enough to play the game freely, then what you have to depend upon for your evaluation of self-worth, are things like winning, money, trophies; you place yourself in the hierarchy of self-worth based on the stuff you're getting.
>
> The ones who seem to be impervious to that content orientation are the ones that really, really love to play the game. And they're going to play the game anyway, and it's great that they get stuff along the way and they're probably not going to deny it, but they don't play the game for the stuff; the money or the name in the paper, they play the game because they love to play the game... I've never seen a person playing for rewards play at the level that those who are playing the game for the sake of the game.
>
> Personal Interview
> Chuck Hogan
> Author, Educator, Performance Specialists

Real play is nonviolent. "Playing to win" for the reward, for recognition is aggressive. Ours is an aggressive culture and this aggressiveness is part of the environment that shapes the synapses of human development. Sensing this aggression, having lost touch with their authentic nature, adulterated adults often become spectators, consumers of commercial entertainment. The lines between play and entertainment get blurred. Professional athletes are entertainers, and most know it. Going to Las Vegas, seeing the shows, feeding the slots feels like play. Adults work so much and so hard that anything that does not feel like work, feels like play. Play to most adults is the unimportant things that happen in between the serious business of making a living. Most adults are, in fact, play deprived.

Our proposal is quite simple. The unique quality of relationship we call play is the optimum relationship for learning, performance and well-being,

Certain ideas arise out of our anxiety and pass from generation to generation. These ideas form anew in each of us as concepts or brain patterns of organization, right along with our general worldview. These concepts influence the accuracy of the actual holonomic (natural) order we should perceive and which consciousness powers through us. The actual order powered to us through consciousness is channeled through, and then warped by, the power of concepts formed in anxiety. Since concepts from anxiety arise from the more powerful subtle realm, our surface awareness and thoughts are shaped by them. We are not consciously aware of these shaping influences, since they are warps in the very power of consciousness giving us our worldview
Bond Of Power

at any age or activity. It is the state, our relationship to an activity that determines if it is play, not the activity. Confusing the activity with the state is a big mistake. Kicking a ball, writing a paper, singing a song, painting the garage floor, nursing a baby, sexual intimacy, almost any activity can be play or work depending on our relationship to it. For most adults play is work.

Abstract Play

Rudolph Steiner spoke of the intense joy in pure abstract thinking. We know mathematicians who experience something akin to the mystical or flow experience while solving or working out solutions. The right answer gives way to the more critical point of elegance of form, the way in which a solution is achieved. Play and creativity are paired from the beginning. Physicists Bohm and Peat suggest that the very essence of thought is play.

Beyond our words, where speech itself is superfluous, a knowing beyond the clouds of all unknowing, an answer beyond all questioning. For here is the catalyst that shapes Eurekas and gives syntheses beyond our mind's wild reach. Here is the catalyst that acts when it has something to catalyze, and always remains unchanged in so doing. Here is the unattainable, that I cannot will or think into my being, falling into my life even as it itself, fleeting, unbelievably, outside all structured thoughts, striving, systems and games. Here all paths are open and synthesized, our freedoms underwritten and assured within.
Crack in the Cosmic Egg

> Creative play is an essential element in forming new hypotheses and ideas. Indeed, thought which tries to avoid play is in fact playing false with itself… The falseness that can creep into the play of thought is shown in the etymology of the words *illusion*, *delusion*, and *collusion*, all of which have as their Latin root *ludere*, "to play." Illusion implies playing false with perception; delusion, playing false with thought; and collusion, playing false together in order to support each other's illusion and delusions.

> Within the act of creative play, fresh perceptions occur which enable a person to propose a new idea that can be put forward for exploration. As the implications of their idea are unfolded, they are composed or put together with other familiar ideas. Eventually the person supposes that these ideas are correct; in other words, he or she makes an assumption or hypothesis and then acts according to the notion that this is the way things actually are. The movement from propose to compose and suppose enables everyday actions to be carried out with little or no conscious thought…. This is appropriate only as long as the mind remains sensitive to the possibility that, in new contexts, evidence may arise that shows that these ideas are wrong or confused. If this happens, scientists [parents, or educators, caregivers, coaches] have to be ready to drop the ideas in question and go back to the free play of thought, out of which may emerge new ideas.

David Bohm, Ph.D. and F. David Peat, Ph.D.

Science, Order and Creativity

This playful relationship with the content of consciousness, the beliefs, images, and values which define our behavior, is at the heart of Optimum Learning Relationships.

Transcendent Play, Sacred Play

Play is fundamentally transcendent. Through play we open the doors of the known to the unknown. What we know implies boundaries. These boundaries shape our behavior, how we learn, what we learn, and how we perform. Rather than living within the boundaries, play extends them. Through athletics we play with physical boundaries: breaking the four-minute mile is a classic example. Walking on fire is another example. We play with emotional boundaries through intimate relationships with other human beings, with animals and with nature. In each case we are playing with "spirit," the true nature-of-our-nature. Bohm believed that the essence of thought is play. Mystical teachers claim the universe is a "play of consciousness." To play is to become again as a little child. And what is it about the child we must become again? Play. Children are closer to their essence, and their essence is play.

Play is not evasion of a grim survival necessity; it is in the service of survival. The animal's survival play centers on mock battle, hunting evasion because these are the specific activities it will employ at maturity for its physical survival. The human child's corresponding activities are imagination, fantasy play and imitation.
Magical Child

The secret of our success in terms of our own development, our personal spiritual journey, is to be in the state of play. To become again as a little child, however, adults must first have fully been a child. For this to take place we must give childhood back to children, which means we must allow them to play. And all they want to do is play, since nature designed their development that way. Play is the way of spirit and truth. All play is sacred.

Rewards & Punishments

Conforming to Expected Patterns

Like love, play is its own reward and not amenable to any form of inner or outer coercion. Remember Mama's smile when she gave us those red cups, her bribe to stop banging on the cupboard door? She was rewarding us for *not doing* something. Her intent behind the smile was to control or modify our behavior. The free, open, and complete involvement in our primary relationship, which a moment ago was a door and hinge, was suddenly replaced by expectation and authority. We discover very early that conforming to predetermined patterns wins rewards from outside authorities. And implied in every reward is the threat we will, in one way or another, be punished if we don't conform. *Primary learning* is transformed into *conditioning* through use of rewards and punishments.

Primary learning is open, free from failure, playful, completely absorbing, and self-rewarding. Primary learning is psychologically safe. It requires no defense. The rewards for participating in the experience are intrinsic, internal, and self generated. Conditioned learning, and what we generally call schooling, imply an external authority, rewards, and potential failure. The goal of conditioning—repetition of predetermined patterns of behavior—is accomplished through the use of external punishments and rewards. Conditioned learning always implies some degree of self-defense. Defensive learning is less efficient than primary learning. The state of potential for failure—not conforming, not obeying, disappointing, frustrating, or enraging the authority—becomes an integral part of the learning experience. Optimum Learning Relationships, the state of flow or being in the Zone are primary experiences. They need no rewards. Complete engagement in the relationship or activity is its own reward.

For most, parenting, education, and business are synonymous with external control maintained with rewards and punishments. The authority, be it mom, dad, caretaker, teacher, coach or instructor, manager or CEO, often justifies and defends controlling behavior by claiming that it is for the child's or employee's own good. Research suggests other motives.

Assumptions about rewards and punishments run deep. They surround us, and are part of our relationships, interwoven in our families, schools, churches, and cherished institutions. No wonder they are so difficult to see. And even more difficult to break free from. Alfie Kohn, in his book *Punished by Rewards*, explores the myth of rewards most of us live by and impose so freely and frequently on our children.

> Behind the practice of presenting a colorful dinosaur sticker to a first grader who stays silent on command is a theory that embodies distinct assumptions about the nature of knowledge, the possibility of choice, and what it means to be a human being...

> It is not the bubble gum itself that is the problem, nor the money, nor the love and attention. The rewards themselves are in some cases innocuous and in other cases indispensable. What concerns me is the practice of using these things as rewards. To take what people want or need and offer it on a contingent basis in order to

Punishments and rage break the child's will, the capacity to overcome obstacles and explore the unknown, which is learning itself. They will leave him with no self-confidence, no faith in himself, and he will fumble or retreat at every little difficulty or challenge... That youngster will grow to be one of us, thinking one thing, feeling another, and acting in a way disconnected from both.
Evolution' End

control how they act—this is where the trouble lies. Our attention is properly focused, in other words, not on "that" (the thing desired) but on the requirement that one must do this in order to get that. Rewarding people for their compliance is not "the way the world works," as many insist. It is not a fundamental law of human nature.

It is but one way of thinking and speaking, of organizing our experience and dealing with others. It may seem natural to us, but it actually reflects a particular ideology that can be questioned. And I believe it is long past time for us to do so.

Alfie Kohn
Punished by Rewards

Rewards are deceptive. We think we are improving spelling, getting the trash taken out, solving a problem, or correcting some form of inappropriate behavior, when the true goal of rewards and punishments is control. And who is most often the beneficiary of control? The controller! To determine the lasting effectiveness of our punishments and rewards we must ask two questions: one, was there a lasting change in behavior and two, was the change brought about for the appropriate reason?

In the short term we can get people to do all sorts of things they might not normally do by providing incentives. Research shows that rewards do not bring about the lasting changes we are hoping for. The negative impact of coercion is not immediately apparent, however. As a result of *our* confusion we continue using rewards; the more we use them the more they seem to be needed. Rewards and punishments are so common, so accepted, and so *normal*, it seems strange to question them. Most people would be offended to hear that rewards are fundamentally dehumanizing. Passing out praise, M&Ms, gold stars, stickers, bonuses, or vacations seems so natural, so civilized. Coercion seems to work well with pets, why not with our children and employees, or so the logic goes.

Repeatedly promising rewards for certain behaviors implies that children and adults would not choose to act responsibly, do good work, love to learn, or perform at extraordinary levels on their own. Mihaly Csikszentmihaly's extensive research into the psychology of optimal experience published in the book *Flow* contradicts this assumption:

> The key element in optimal experience is that it is an end in itself… it is a self-contained activity, one that is not done with the expecta-

Our sociability is instinctual and arises spontaneously of its own. Culture is intellectual, arbitrary, and must be induced, injected or enforced. Sociability is learning in its most complete form and breeds reflective thought. Enculturation is conditioning and enhancement of automatic reflexes. A society is made of spontaneous nurturing and love while culture is subtly hated, rebelled against sooner or later, subtly or flagrantly, if not in the terrible two's then in the terrible teens. And such rebellions are forcibly put down through pain, fear, guilt and shame, or the rebel simply put away out of sight.
The Biology of Transcendence

tion of some future benefit, the doing itself is the reward. When experience is intrinsically rewarding, life is justified in the present, instead of being held hostage to a hypothetical future gain... The solution is to gradually become free of societal rewards and learn how to substitute for them rewards that are under one's own powers.

Mihaly Csikszentmihaly
Flow, the Psychology of Optimal Experience

Controlling another implies unequal status:

If rewards not only reflect differences in power but also contribute to them, it should not be surprising that their use may benefit the more powerful party—that is, the rewarder. This point would seem almost too obvious to bother mentioning except for the fact that, in practice, rewards are typically justified as being in the interest of the individual receiving them. We claim to reinforce people to teach them things they need to be taught. But one writer, after ticking off the specific objectives of behavior modification programs, asks, "In whose interest is it for a prisoner, a student, or a patient to be less complaining, more attentive, submissive, and willing to work?" Who really benefits when a child quiets down and sits still?

Alfie Kohn
Punished by Rewards

Kohn and Csikszentmihaly agree that rewards bolster the traditional order of things. "To de-emphasize conventional rewards threatens the existing power structure," be it in the family, classroom, or on the job. Those in control like being in control. Take away authority and control and most parents get nervous. It is difficult for many teachers to imagine replacing authority with mutual respect and deep communication. It takes too much time and attention. Frequent use and widespread acceptance of punishments and rewards mask their failure to bring about lasting change. Kohn lists five reasons why rewards have no place in optimum learning relationships:

1. Rewards Punish:

Controlling by seduction (rewards) is every bit as controlling as control by threat (punishment). Both represent a psychological model that conceives of motivation in terms of behavior modification.

2. Rewards Rupture Relationships:

The ability to reward and punish implies authority, power, and control. One person has the power, the other doe not. This imbalance prevents the positive relationships that promote optimal learning and performance.

3. Rewards Ignore Reasons:

Rewards draw attention away from root causes. The rewarder does not have to deal with the source of the trouble.

4. Rewards Discourage Risk-Taking:

Rewards undermine creativity and innovation. They are the enemies of exploration. When rewards are offered, people do exactly what is necessary to get the prize and nothing more.

5. External Rewards Reduce Internal Motivation:

Rewards tend to make people dependent on external, rather than self-generated incentives, and change how we feel about activities we may naturally enjoy. "A single onetime reward for doing something you used to enjoy can kill your interest in it for weeks."

Adults take control when they organize child's play. Adults become the authority. Praise and blame point the way down predetermined paths. Independent thinking, authentic interest, innate curiosity, and true creativity are often out-of-bounds. The ratio of "no" to "yes" is seventeen to one in favor of "no." Often the more intelligent and adventuresome the child, the more extreme the pressure to conform.

It Is All About Control

Children learn very early to mold themselves in ways they hope will win the approval of mom, dad, and mentors. They attempt to control the controllers by pleasing, doing the expected, conforming to safe patterns. The good baby is the quiet baby. The over-achiever is looked upon as the well-socialized child, the one most likely to succeed. Failing to win the approval, some children rebel. Others withdraw.

With increasing frequency, those who do not color between the lines, those who are restless in school and not so easy to control, are diagnosed with attention disorders and medicated. The widespread use of prescription drugs by preschool-age children for mental and emotional disorders has no historical precedent.

Our reptilian brain is skilled in deceptive procedures, developed eons ago to deceive predators. We can change our color, so to speak, like a chameleon, according to social environment. We are quite capable of being not just two-faced, but multifaceted like a politician or lawyer, particularly if we feel threatened in any way. We also use this deceptive skill on behalf of our high brain's strategies for winning in the deceptive world of folly, (commerce and politics for instance) and our high brain will skillfully rationalize and make morally respectable, at least to ourselves, our often quite immoral actions. Through our high brain's alliance with this deceptive low brain, we learn to lie, gloating and gleeful when successfully deceiving, lamenting and self-pitying when so deceived.
The Biology of Transcendence

Treating attention-deficit/hyperactivity disorder (ADHD) has become a multibillion-dollar industry. Drug companies are launching brand-name ads for ADHD drugs in women's magazines and on network television. These ads break a thirty-year-old agreement between the international community and the pharmaceutical industry not to market controlled drugs directly to consumers. Between May of 2000 and May of 2001, more than 20.5 million prescriptions were written for ADHD drugs, up 37 percent over the past five years. Stimulants used to treat ADHD are classified by the Drug Enforcement Agency as Schedule II drugs, the most highly addictive drugs that are still legal. ADHD drugs are among today's most frequently stolen prescriptions and most-abused legal drugs. In some U.S. communities, 20 percent of children, beginning with preschoolers, are taking stimulants. Most abusers, DEA officials say, are kids. Most dealers are kids who are prescribed the drugs to treat ADHD. Direct-to-consumer marketing by drug companies in popular media creates strong pressure to drug children. We forget that drug pushers are drug pushers. What do we expect? The real issue is control.

A cover story in *Time Magazine* described children who are out of control. Read between the lines and we discover that parents are out of control with their use of rewards and punishments, contests, grades, and competition strategies. The more rewards are used, the less effective they become. What goes around comes around. The controlled eventually become the controllers.

Our Contest Culture

To be free of guilt and at one with the universal system is to be free of anxiety—and you can threaten and control man only through his anxiety. So the forces of social-political control must always induce and maintain that anxiety.
Bond of Power

We have turned everything into a contest. Schools are based on comparison—tests and grades. In business our worth is measured by the bottom line. My child learned to walk sooner than yours. My grade point average is higher than yours. Children discover very early that the score is *very* important. How they feel about themselves is based most often on performance—on the score. Behind our contests and comparisons is a strong belief that the important things in life, the prestige, awards, money, and love, all the things we value, are limited, and therefore must be competed for. The miracle of being human is not enough. We must prove ourselves by winning the approval of others. Life is a contest. A few win. Most do not.

We assume that the only way to survive is by competing. Everyone compares himself with everyone else. Self-worth is measured in terms of external future goals. We see it in the family, our school, in business, church, the military, and neighborhood street gangs. The entire culture operates on the assumption that "more for me equals less for you." We assume very early that our real self, who we really are, is defined by the limited goods, the services, and prestige the culture provides through contests. By competing we buy into a cultural identity that masks our true nature. We become attached to this cultural identity and all the rewards reinforce that image. The culture controls us through that image. If we did not identify with that image, the culture would find it very difficult to control us. That is what the rewards and contests do. They provide a way for culture to control us. Optimum states of learning and performance liberate us from the image and from culture's control. Suddenly what seemed miraculous becomes easy, even natural.

> This cultural identity is very important because, in a contest culture, most people lose. That is part of the control, but we don't tell anybody that. When we stop winning, as certain athletes and stars have discovered, we find that the culture never liked who we really are. What the culture likes is the illusion of being a winner. Who inhabits this position is totally irrelevant.

Personal Interview
O. Fred Donaldson, Ph.D.
Author, <u>*Playing by Heart*</u>

It is not too difficult to see that rewards are used to control behavior and that the real beneficiary of the control is the controller. Early identification with an external identity gives the existing parental, educational, religious, business, and political structure the power to control behavior in the predetermined patterns that support the existing structure we call culture. We enter contests to prove how well we can conform and by so doing win the favor of others. We enter that state of optimum experience, play, flow, or the Zone when the false limitations, conflicts, and pressures of this cultural identity disappear. For that timeless moment there is a "crack in the cosmic egg." Culture loses control of us and we are free to break the four-minute mile. We can run, jump, hit the ball, climb the mountain, think, imagine, and dream in completely new ways. We are in play—in the Zone—and literally have slipped out of culture's control. To risk being that out of control, we must feel very safe.

As of this writing (1996-2001), failure of nurturing has led to an average of eighteen children per day in the United States struck by bullets from other children's guns.
Six thousand a year die from those wounds.
The rising inability of our young people to modify primitive impulses and behaviors has become virtually a national security matter and we can't seem to build prisons fast enough.
We have thirteen- and fourteen-year-old children, boys and girls, in penitentiaries.
Sixteen year old girls have babies in prison under horrifying, bestial conditions. To say the least, our "socializing" tactics are working poorly for our wounded society.
The Biology of Transcendence

A positive emotional state entrains or unites our systems for thought, feeling, and action, shifts our concentration and energy toward support of our intellectual creative forebrain, and we both learn and remember easily. In infant-children, the mother's emotional state determines the child's state, and therefore development in general. On the other hand, and this is true lifelong, any kind of negative response, any form of fear or anger of any sort, shifts our attention-energy from evolution's latest intellectual to her earliest survival brain. We then don't have full access to evolution's higher intelligence, but react on the more primitive level. When we are insecure, anxious, undecided and tense, attention can get divided among the three brains, each with its own agenda... In this all-too-common confusion, learning and development are impaired in children and decision-making can be very faulty in adults.
The Biology of Transcendence

The genius of play is not being limited by all the categories in which we live. In that unique time/space which is play, we're not members of those categories. We aren't men or women, white or black, Americans or South Africans. By categories I mean the social, cultural, psychological image that I identify as being Fred, white, male, 6'4", 200-pound athlete. Play is nature's energy, not Fred's. I didn't invent it. I don't create it. I can participate in it. I can share in it. I can allow it. And only to the extent that the social categories disappear can play happen.

Personal Interview
O. Fred Donaldson, Ph.D.
Author, *Playing by Heart*

Any image we hold about ourselves—and therefore defend—is, by definition, limited. How could it be otherwise? The universe is always changing and so are we. The more fixed and rigid the image, the more confining are its boundaries. The more flexible or expansive the image, the greater the range of possibilities that image may accommodate. Having no image implies real freedom and unlimited possibilities. If there is no image we can be anything. This implies a quality of relationship that is very difficult to predict and control. So why aren't more of us in the Zone most of the time?

Approval of Others

Membership in the group is very important. Human babies are born nine months premature compared to other species. Acceptance and approval of others is a matter of survival. We must live within the boundaries the culture provides. All organizations within the culture operate by the same basic rules. We are accepted and considered good if we abide by the terms of membership. We pay allegiance to the group by conforming to its accepted pattern. This often involves contests. If we stop paying allegiance, stop competing, we are not a member anymore. And that is very scary.

Everybody knows how to complete the sentence. There's only one way of doing things, the right way. Anything worth doing is worth doing right. If you can't do it right, don't do it at all. As parents we show the world how adequate we are through the performance of our children. We focus on their behavior and their behavior is a reflection of our competency as parents. And as children learn they are going to make mistakes. We know how to celebrate our victories but not our defeats, losses, mistakes, and failures. We don't know how to celebrate the learning that's earned through the mistake-making process. We tend to cover them up and not share them with each other. That's the way the culture functions.

Personal Interview
Bowen White, M.D.
Author, Clown

What Will They Think of Me?

If it is a tight game and this shot really matters, most of us get nervous. People are more afraid of public speaking than of dying. What will others think of us if we strike out or say something stupid? That is the big question, isn't it? We are afraid of what others may think. At that crucial instant our attention splits between meeting the challenge and looking good. Self-defense always comes first. The greater the fear the greater the energy that goes into defense. And it is this split that separates most of us from the truly great performers. When the pressure is on, the great athletes, the great dancers, the great anything, forget about themselves and meet the challenge completely with one hundred percent of their energy and attention. Love of the game, love of experience, love of this present moment and all its relationships can occur only when we feel safe enough to play, when we no longer feel any need to justify or defend ourselves. If we are being judged, tested, compared, or graded, the true intelligence of play is denied.

> Contests are everywhere, in the street gang, the Little League team, the professional team, in school, in the corporation. In a contest culture we end up competing with the entire world. There's no time-out. Parents are part of their peer group hierarchy, which extends to their children. We think we will be failures if we don't compete in our religion, in our job, our marriage, in child-rearing, in the car we drive, and we pass this on to our children very early.

> It all starts when we substitute original play with cultural/competitive games at home or on the playground. When this happens, the rules change from sharing to not sharing and we aren't honest with children about this. We don't say, "Remember that sharing I told you about in pre-school, well now in first grade we don't do that anymore. Forget the sharing stuff. Now it's winning that counts."

> When original play is traded for competition, the incredibly resilient, flexible, creative beings children are become trapped in the

Culture exists only as a process of correcting the error of its own existence, which existence causes us pain and anguish while impelling us to correct our culture to escape that very pain. In the enormous consumption of energy culture must have for its error ridden sustenance, not one mind, not one soul, can be spared. (And should you try to bring up your child for any other purpose than supporting culture, your culture will turn and rend you, in politically appropriate ways; so you best keep quiet about it should you try.)
The Biology of Transcendence

contest. From then on, most of their creative energy is used in ways that insure they don't fail. Risking anything new becomes too tough.

Whether they are a seven-year-old, worried about how he or she looks on the street, or the man or woman caught in a horrible job, they are trapped and the contest doesn't allow them to step out. To not compete means you're off the team, no longer a member, you're an outsider, all alone. That's the cultural trap. Not only is the child involved in that hierarchy, the parent is too. Each of us is like a knot in a fishing net. You're going to be a failure if you don't compete in your religion, in your job, in your marriage, in your child-rearing, in the car and home you have, and we pass this on to our children very early.

Personal Interview
O. Fred Donaldson, Ph.D.
Author, *Playing by Heart*

> *Using our intellect defensively we function in an anti-evolutionary mode: Our neuocortical system serves our lowest and most primitive structures.*
> *The open universe available to us through that highest system closes down at that point to the tight confines of our ancient R-system (core or reptilian brain). Our already selective brain selects more rigidly than ever, discarding all signals except those strengthening that primitive defense system. Our world itself is a threat and we become like William Blake's "armed crustaceans eternally on the alert."*
> Evolution's End

Parents say, "What do you want me to do? It's a jungle out there. If I don't teach my child to be a strong competitor he or she will get creamed. Survival of the fittest. I win, you lose." CEOs lament, "I had to lay off half of our workforce to save the company." Gang members say the same thing. "I had to kill to be a member." Many preschools have entrance exams and waiting lists. Replacing child's play with adult-organized athletic programs, nationwide "high stakes" testing, corporate brand identification, and other pressures insures that everyone is a competitor. The truth is, Darwin was wrong.

Research has shown that human nature—and all of nature—is really cooperative. The term "survival of the fittest" was coined by Herbert Spencer, a sociologist, and was a very unsound view of what Darwin was saying. In the 19th century, which was called the "age of conflict," competition was the principle by which most imperialist nations lived and competition was readily accepted, joyfully by the military of every country…

The very origin of life is associated with cooperation. If you study ameba and take one cell and place it on one end of a slide and another cell on the other, and observe what happens, both tend to migrate toward each other. This I believe is the basic pattern of all living forms. It's right there in the nature of your protoplasm. And then we develop two cells, four cells, and these endear together into millions of cells, all of which are in cooperation with each other. This is the biological basis of all living things, a cooperative behavior, which binds the society more closely together. We are born to live as if to live and love were one.

Personal Interview
Ashley Montagu
Author, Educator, Humanist

Play Deprivation & Violence

Stuart Brown has spent most of his professional life exploring play, in humans and in nature. He wrote a cover story on animals and play for <u>National Geographic</u> and a PBS special on the same theme. The critical need for play and the violence associated with play depravation emerged as a surprise finding in his investigation into the life of Charles Whitman, the Texas Tower Sniper.

I got a call from my chief of service saying that I was to organize an investigation and find out why a twenty-five-year-old man, who by then had been identified as Charles Whitman, would shoot thirty-one people, killing nineteen, off the Texas University tower. This was 1966, three years after the Kennedy motorcade and Governor Conley wanted to know what would produce this kind of tragedy. So we organized a team and studied Whitman's life.

Within a week interviews with family and friends began to tell the story. He'd been an over-controlled, humiliated kid. He came from a tightly knit Catholic family. Charles was very bright, youngest Eagle Scout in the United States, an altar boy, in ROTC, was a scholarship recipient, married a delightful woman, and it looked like he had everything going for him. What came out of the personal interviews however, was that he had not ever engaged in spontaneous play.

The next year I headed a team that went throughout the prison and the state hospital systems to interview all the young male murderers in the state of Texas. Over 90 percent of the murderers, whether they came from upper-class economic circumstances or were in a state hospital system revealed high levels of play deprivation.

If the adult culture is play-deprived, which is pervasive in Western Europe and the United States, then that adult culture is not going to allow the natural evolution of authentic play to develop in children. We see this all around us. Spontaneous free play in childhood has

To the epidemic of children shooting children, add the increase of child suicide. Up to the post World-War II period, no suicide had ever been recorded under age fourteen. By 1991 child suicide extended down to age three and a child attempted suicide in our country every 78 seconds. Some six a day succeeded. Suicide as of the year 2000 is now the third highest cause of all deaths in children between the ages of five and seventeen. Far more suicides are attempted by girls than boys, yet boys far outnumber girls in actual completed suicide. There is no historical precedent of this phenomena at all, and it is almost totally ignored. While one hears the constant shrill commands of NO! and DON'T at every hand, from cradle to grave, seldom do we see nurturance and love. The price of arbitrary compliance from the toddler with our own shameful action is paid over and over, year after year, by our whole nation.
The Biology of Transcendence

been systematically replaced by adult organized activities.

Personal Interview
Stuart Brown, M.D.
Author, PBS Producer

Focusing on the Score

A negative experience of any sort, whether an event in our environ-ment or simply a thought in our head, brings an automatic shift of attention-energy from forebrain to hindbrain; that is, away from our high intellec-tual verbal brain toward the lower R-system and its defenses. This shift short-changes our intellect, cripples our learning and memory, and can lock our high forebrain into service of and identification with our lowest hind-brain. (Perhaps this explains the rather reptilian nature of your boss or in-law.)

The Biology of Translucence

Something deeper and more fundamental is at stake than gold stars, M&Ms, blue ribbons, and report cards. We learn very early to identify ourselves with our performance, with the score. We've been praised and shamed into believing that great performances equal a great person. We feel good about ourselves when we hit a home run and lousy when we strike out. Relationships are mirrors. As we interact with the world we catch glimpses of ourselves reflected in the eyes of the people we love. Spilling our milk or wetting our pants gets a stern look, a "No! Bad boy or girl," perhaps even a yank on the arm or a swat across the britches. World-class golfer Peter Jacobsen discovered the meaning of "the score" from a child while coaching a junior basketball game.

I was keeping score and my son's team scored fifteen baskets the first half and the other team scored two baskets. It was a white-wash. Our team was throwing the ball in, lay-ups, back and forth. The other team rarely had the ball and rarely scored. The buzzer went off for the first half. Kids come charging over to me and the coach is giving them high five, "Way to go, way to go," and the kids come up to me and they say, "Mr. Jacobson, what's the score?" And I say, "Well, it's thirty to four," and they said, "Who's win-ning?" Now if you think about that, it was obvious to everybody who was winning, the coaches, the parents, because they were scoring so many baskets here and none there. But if you stop and think about the children, score had meant nothing to them. They were playing the game. The only reason these kids keep score in these games is for the parent's and coach's satisfaction. Who cares? They're ten years old.

Personal Interview
Peter Jacobsen
PGA Tour Champion

Whacking, Spanking & Corporal Punishment

Rewards and punishments, keeping score, tests and grades are all forms of behavior modification, social conditioning, and control. They have no place in optimum states of peak performance, learning, or wellness. The research behind this statement is persuasive. Yet old habits, especially those justified and defended by strong cultural or religious traditions, persist: "Spare the rod and spoil the child."

In the United States almost 400,000 children are subjected to corporal punishment in schools each year in the 23 states that allow it: Alabama, Arizona, Arkansas, Colorado, Delaware, Florida, Georgia, Idaho, Indiana, Kansas, Kentucky, Louisiana, Mississippi, Missouri, New Mexico, North Carolina, Ohio, Oklahoma, Pennsylvania, South Dakota, Tennessee, Texas, and Wyoming.

The federal government prohibits physical punishment to train animals under the Animal Welfare Act, the Horse Protection Act and other laws. The Attorney General, in releasing the latest statistics on violence in schools, said "all children should be able to go to school safe from violence." Hitting children *IS* violence. Are school children any less deserving of protection than animals?

Today, not one country in Europe permits teachers to batter pupils. In recent months many places in the developing world have followed Europe's good example. School corporal punishment is now illegal in Kenya, Punjab (Pakistan), Delhi (India), Trinidad, Tobago, and Thailand, to name a few.

The trend against spanking is extending even beyond the classroom. In 1978, Sweden became the first nation to give children the same protection against assault and battery that is enjoyed by every other class of citizen. Austria, Croatia, Cyprus, Denmark, Finland, Israel, Italy, Latvia, Germany, and Norway banned parental spanking. Movements in England, Canada, Australia, and New Zealand to prohibit parental spanking are gaining strength, and inevitably these four will join the others.

A growing number of experts believe that children in general and girls in particular, should not be spanked at home or subjected to corporal punishment at school. Experts say such spankings can precondition girls to accept violence and boys to rely on it. All studies show that boys are spanked significantly more than girls, but there are special concerns with girls who are spanked. Of particular concern is the sexual aspect of spanking..

It is important to acknowledge, say the experts, that hitting a child does not work any better than alternative methods. Corporal punishment has harmful side effects that can include juvenile delinquency, domestic abuse, and depression. "When you put those things together, you can see that corporal

The assumption runs like this: In this 3 billion years of experimenting, life has evolved our huge and brilliant mind-brain system in order that we might have the intelligence to outwit and so survive this life system that has evolved us. That is, we really believe that we have a superior brain in order to survive her. Outwitting means acting against, dominating, overcoming, removing the causes of stress... Would a 3-billion-year experiment in genetic coding really have produced as its finest product a brain whose only purpose is to outwit itself?
Magical Child

All of us know intuitively that we are not by nature savage beasts. Fewer are aware that we are driven to some fairly beastly behaviors by enculturation, which procedure is supposed to do just the opposite. This irony brings us to the fundamental struggle between society and culture, which is also the struggle between intelligence and intellect, evolution and devolution, spirit and religion, gospel and myth, heart and brain, love and law, creator with created.

The Biology of Transcendence

punishment should be avoided," says Murray A. Straus, professor of sociology at the University of New Hampshire and co-director of that school's Family Research Laboratory. "It's all part of a cycle of violence—loss of self esteem, accepting violent behavior," she says. "The more children are spanked, the more likely they are to engage in digressive behaviors."

Jordan Riak, Executive Director, *Parents and Teachers Against Violence in Education,* Project NoSpank at *www.nospank.org*, makes an analogy between domestic violence and spanking and urges the nation's women's rights organizations to take up the issue. "Just as we as a society no longer condone a man striking his wife," he says, "we as a society should no longer condone the striking of our children, especially our daughters."

Should corporal punishment be allowed or banished (at home and) in schools? Ralph S. Welsh, Ph.D., and member, Advisory Board of The Center for the Study of Corporal Punishment and Issues in the Schools at Temple University, argues: "After 25 years of research into the relationship between corporal punishment and delinquency, the answer is a no-brainer." Welsh found the following:

After evaluating thousands of delinquent boys and girls, and exhaustively personally interviewing their parents, I am totally convinced that no one can have a violent child without beating him/her.

- The degree of violence seen in delinquents is highly correlated with the amount and severity of physical parental punishment they received growing up. The recidivist male delinquent who has never been hit with a belt, board, cord or fist, is nearly nonexistent. All of the major assassins of the world were victims of the belt—Joseph Stalin, Adolph Hitler, Sirhan Sirhan, James Earl Ray, and Arthur Bremmer, just to name a few; Joseph Stalin, perhaps the worst butcher of our time, was a known battered child.

- Corporal punishment can only work through the inculcation of fear. When the fear wears off, anger is left in its place. Nearly every parent who hits was hit as a child themselves, and insists that a good old-fashioned whack on the rear doesn't do anyone any harm; not true.

- Every whack results in sensory desensitization (partly through the beta endorphin system, and partly through adaptation to pain) and adds a little anger to the system; when the child becomes insensitive to the beatings (nearly all of my delinquent kids would rather be beaten than grounded), he/she becomes blunted to the hurt of others (including the parents) and needs additional stimulus input through the use of drugs or reckless thrill-seeking behavior.

• Hitting children in the school, to insure good discipline is not only idiotic, it is a dangerous example to others. It is no surprise that the states that held on to corporal punishment in the school-room the longest were those states with the highest rates of violence.

• The aggressive Type A (cardiac prone) individual is more commonly a childhood victim of the belt; high blood pressure is more common in those who cannot effectively control their anger, and we find they, too, are more often former children of the belt.

• Teens who threaten suicide are often physically mistreated kids who are unable to turn their anger outward, so they turn it inward on themselves; kids who are beaten, especially girls, are at high risk for making suicidal gestures.

It is very difficult to see the connection between spanking a child and rewarding them with Gummi Bears, gold stars, trophies and graduate degrees, but the link is there. As we reach out and touch the world it slowly begins to tell us who we are and whether or not it approves of us by these measures. Day by day we accept the image we see reflected in the mirror of our relationships. People may talk about unconditional love and acceptance, but that is not what children see. Children see our punishments and rewards, our comparisons, judgments, and contests. Rewards imply comparison and comparisons lead ever-so-easily to contests. Contests, like rewards, are a tender trap: they seduce us into compliance. So early is our identification with external values that few ever discover or identify their authentic nature, their true self-worth. They can not take the time. They are too busy competing in a contest culture.

Athletics & the Intelligence of Play

Adulterating Free-play

The original play many adults remember as children has slipped away. Neighborhood pick-up games have all but disappeared. Today it is front and center, everyone is watching, try-outs, uniforms, grown-up rules and regulations.

The ability to play on the surface depends on the success of the work beneath, which depends on the success of the play. When play on the surface is finally destroyed and work on the surface become the aware self's drive, the inner work of intelligence breaks down, and the synergy of the system collapses. Anxiety takes over, joy disappears, and the avoidance of death becomes the central issue of life.
That is we grow up.
Magical Child

Somewhere after World War II, society suddenly had no room for children, our quiet childhood streets, filled with speeding autos; yards were status symbols, and children's play was relegated to playgrounds with professional playground supervisors. Supervised play replaced child play. Adult rules, regulations, and decisions began to replace our passionately defended personal criteria and judgments... Gone were the choosing up of sides, the striving for fairness, arguing the rules and infringements, the heated hammering out of decisions. Everything was managed by adults; they created the teams and provided the uniforms, which of course soon carried advertisements of "sponsors." Children stood, grim-faced and serious while parents on the sidelines shouted invectives for victory at all costs. This new child carried the team, sponsor, parents, and social image on his or her shoulders into every victory or defeat.

Evolution's End

Fanned by the television images of professional ball players reaping multi-year, multimillion-dollar contracts and by fear of unsupervised neighborhood activities, today millions of moms, dads, kids, and coaches are involved in adult-organized athletic programs. The pressure to join a team is immense. To not participate means not being a member, a heavy price to pay in a contest culture. Most do so because athletics holds the promise of enriching and expanding human development, developing self-discipline, team spirit, cooperation, loyalty, and self-esteem.

Sports are a western yoga. At its core, when pursued with passion and for its own sake, sport becomes a transformative practice. The problem is, for most athletes in the West, there is no philosophy, no psychology, no context in which to understand sports in this larger dimension. We're like the little Lilliputians who have chained the Gulliver in us down, and in sports, Gulliver gets loose for a few minutes. Our challenge is to bring sports into alignment with this larger being in us that's trying to manifest.

Personal Interview
Michael Murphy
Founder, Eselan Institute, Author, *In the Zone, Future of the Body*

This larger context is overshadowed by the contest culture. For the vast majority the promise of optimum development is broken very early. Few ever experience the Zone. A recent headline in *USA Today*, "Tiger Woods Wins the War," tells the story, not of personal transformation, but of the lessons most young players learn in organized athletic programs: conflict, comparison, win-lose, less for you means more for me.

Many have heard the famous phrase, "On the playing fields of Eton Britain's battles were won." Eton is the premiere private school of Great Britain. On its playing fields Britain's elite young men were trained in rugby and football. The character formed by this experience was given credit for victories in battles waged for the Queen, principally Napoleon's defeat at Waterloo. Myths aside, athletics teaches young people how to compete.

I played Little League baseball, high school football, college crew, amateur ski racing. I competed as a university person and never knew there was anything else. The whole world seemed that way.

When I looked at the wildlife programs on National Geographic, and they said baby lions were playing in order to become predators, I said, "Yeah, that makes sense."

Had I not played with wolves and cheetahs, I would never have understood that animals know another kind of play. They know contest, but there's another dimension that I call original play that most of us never see. It's invisible in a contest culture. We have been programmed for so long, not only as Americans, but as human beings, to believe that fight/flight, survival of the fittest, and competition is the only way to be.

When you experience that love and belonging are the most important things, not just as an idea, not just to be nice, but in a very tangible way, the question becomes, how do I live that way, moment by moment? That experience changes everything. Once you're safe and not dissipating your energy in self-defense, then it's much easier to communicate, to love, to be kind and do all those things that we'd really rather do than hurt and defend. This is what original play is all about.

The most important thing I've experienced through play, over the past twenty-five years, is that I "belong" to the universe. It is that sense of belonging that I've learned. And that has allowed me to learn the essence of all the things that we think of as separate, like the essence of a lion, or a child, or a Zulu person, or a flower, all of that. By learning that we all belong, I'm no longer afraid of the differences. Differences are there for me to learn how to be fully human and to share that with every other form on earth. That's very powerful and it literally places me in the midst of the universe.

Personal Interview

O. Fred Donaldson, Ph.D.
Author, *Playing by Heart*

When asked why children should participate in athletic programs, adults often say that sports is a metaphor for life, that it teaches children how to be team players and how to win and lose gracefully. Many believe that competition builds character. Contrary to popular belief, amateur athletics does not often lead to optimum learning or performance.

A Lewis Harris poll showed that 50 percent of American kids experience their first major failure in life in sports. Some kids can climb the ropes. Some kids can't. Climbing the rope is a public event and if you can't, there's a humiliation factor, which can affect a child for the rest of his or her life. Some kids get what I call the Wednesday morning disease where they just don't want to go

Schore describes how each prohibiting NO! or shaming look brings a shock of threat, interrupts the will to explore and learn, and produces a cascade of negative hormonal-neural reactions in the child. Schore describes the infant-toddler's depressive state brought about through these episodes of "shame-stress." The confusion and depression in the child comes from two powerful encoded directives: First, maintain the bond with the caretaker at all costs. Second: explore the world and build a knowledge of it, also at all costs. Throughout history the caretaker was the major support, mentor and guide in the toddler's world-body exploration and learning. When the child, driven by nature's imperative to explore his or her world, is threatened if he does so by the care giver - with whom he is equally driven to maintain the bond - the contradiction is profound. The resulting ambiguity sets up the first major wedge in that toddler mind, a wedge that finally becomes a gaping chasm.
The Biology of Transcendence

Bonding is a nonverbal form of psychological communication, an intuitive rapport that operates outside of or beyond ordinary rational, linear ways of thinking and perceiving. Bonding involves what I call primary processing, a biological function of enormous practical value, yet largely lost to technological man.

Magical Child

to gym class. I used to think they all had dental appointments. In reality, they were scared to death of coming to that class.

Personal Interview
John Douillard
Author, *Body, Mind & Sport*

I played sports as a kid. I had coaches humiliate me in front of my teammates and reinforce my feelings of inadequacy. That did not help me access and express giftedness. I don't think I was nearly as good as I could have been if someone would have been more supportive of me and less critical. That would have been wonderful.

Personal Interview
Bowen White, M.D.
Author, Educator, Clown

People get uptight because they are afraid of failing. They're afraid of what folks are going to say, of being criticized. My dad was a perfectionist. He was very critical. If I could do anything over again I would have him be more supportive so I'd feel like it was okay to go out and make a mistake. I didn't want to come home from a basketball game and hear how I didn't do this or didn't do that. It'd be more fun to be able to play and not worry about being criticized when you got home. I always liked other kids who would go out and just play freely with no fear of making a mistake and I'd say man, I wish I could play like that. It wasn't until the last three or four years that I really started to overcome what it took all those years to build up. It's a tough barrier to overcome.

Personal Interview
Tom Lehman, PGA
Winner, British Open

Intrinsic (Inside) vs. Extrinsic (Outside) Motivation

It is not the activity, but the motivation (why we do what we do) that determines the meaning of an experience. Swinging a bat to see how far a ball can fly and swinging to "beat" another person or group are very different motivations, very different states of relationship. Motivation affects the state, which alters the meaning of the experience. Motivation shapes content; it shapes what we see and learn and how we relate. When adults transform child's play into contests they alter the reason children participate in the activity. They change the meaning of the experience.

The vast majority of learning occurs naturally each time we interact with the environment. We do not interact to learn. The interaction is the learning. Eating and breathing are part of our nature. So is learning. The motivation for this natural (primary) learning is *intrinsic*. It comes from within.

There is another motivation for learning: *Extrinsic* motivation is that which comes from outside. Winning parental approval or the approval of others is an external reason to learn or behave in a certain way. Being popular is an external motivation for wearing designer jeans. Getting straight A's in math, if we hate math, is externally motivated. Getting straight A's in math because we love the challenge of solving problems is intrinsically motivated. If we love an activity we do it because we love doing it, not because we are going to get good grade. It is not the behavior or the activity that matters; it is why we do what we do that counts.

The motivation that leads to optimum learning and performance always comes from within. We excel because we love to do what we do. We love the learning that *is* the activity. Optimum learning *is* optimum performance. Optimum performance *is* optimum learning. Performance and learning are two ways of describing the same action. Here are some other reasons parents believe competitive sports are good for their children (beyond sports simply being a metaphor for life). Note if the motivation is intrinsic or extrinsic and who benefits the most from the list.

- To keep them occupied, off the street, and away from drugs.
  (External/Fear/Control)
- Because it is safe. I know what they are doing.
  (External/Fear/Control)
- Athletic programs are supervised by adults.
  (External/Fear/Control)
- Socialization; children learn how to be part of a team.
  (External/Comparison/Competition)
- So he/she can make it in life, be successful.
  (External/Fear/ Competition)
- I loved sports as a child; he/she will too.
  (External/Comparison/Control)
- He/she needs to develop their natural talent;
  starting early is better.
  (External/Comparison/Control)
- Being a winner means being popular.

Evolution's intent for us lies far beyond exercises of "mind over matter," though we need to know of such capacities. Our job on earth is not to mutilate our earth matrix, but to nurture and maintain her as she nurtures and maintains us. We need to develop the intelligences needed to go beyond this matrix before we are buried under it. The sage changes nothing but hearts and minds. A truly mature society would leave few traces of itself. On reaching such a maturity that we could willfully change our "ontological constructs" (miracles in the classical sense), we would have no inclination to perform them, as there are far greater themes in evolution's score.
Evolution's End

Bonding is a psychological-biological state, a vital physical link that coordinates and unifies the entire biological system. Bonding seals a primary knowing that is the basis for rational thought. We never are conscious of being bonded; we are conscious only of our acute disease when we are not bonded, or when we are bonded to compulsion and material things. (Linus with is security blanket, in the comic strip "Peanuts" is the tragicomic symbol of this.) The unbonded person (and bonding to objects is to be very much unbonded in a functional sense) will spend his/her life in a search for what bonding was designed to give; the matrix. The intelligence can never unfold as designed because it never gets beyond this primal need. All intellectual activity, no matter how developed, will be used in a search for that matrix, which will take on such guises as authenticity, making it in this world, getting somewhere.

Magical Child

(External/Comparison/ Competition)
- It is better than television and video games.
  (Fear/Control)
- Kids need exercise—it gets them outside.
  (Fear/Control)
- Everyone else is doing it—he/she will be left out.
  (External/Comparison/Control/ Competition)
- His/her older brother/sister was a great player.
  (External/Comparison/Control)
- Kids are lazy—they need discipline.
  (External/Control)
- Kids need strong male role models (the coach).
  (External/Control)
- It teaches them how to follow rules.
  (External/Control)
- Look at all the money and attention athletes get.
  (External/Comparison)
- It builds self-esteem.
  (External/Comparison)

Each item draws attention to a concern parents have about their children. As we discovered with rewards and punishments, these motivators are deceptive. By talking about the child, we lose track of the simple fact that these are adult issues. The list would look very different had we asked children to share what they think.

When intrinsically motivated, love of the experience and learning are their own rewards. Attention is so complete and "in the moment" that there is no energy left over to create an image of self, good or bad. When externally motivated, which implies being judged, we fail to achieve this complete *entrained* attention. The judgment—the score—demands its own attention. It is the attention given to the score that creates the image.

Good self-images and poor self-images are equally defensive. We tend to believe that good self-images are desirable, like rewards. Rewards imply punishments. A good self-image is as defensive as a bad one.

Maintaining any image, good or bad, demands energy, and it is this attention that separates the truly great performers from the rest of us. Great performers meet the moment with complete attention. The greater the energy with which we meet the challenge, the better the score. Defending a self-image, good or bad, is a waste of energy. If adults are preoccupied justifying and defending their self-images, that is what children will do. If adults are externally motivated, children will be externally motivated. If adults are experiencing and expressing joy in the moment, so will children. That's just about as complicated as it gets.

Following the Leader

Children are compelled by nature to follow the model set for them by adults and the adult culture. A theme that we will return to again and again, especially in section two, is the need for adults to share optimum learning states with children. Optimum learning and performance have three primary characteristics: intrinsic-self motivation, love of the experience, and learning. None of these qualities are "modeled" when parents enroll their children in Little League.

> Kids always wanted to play, they always got together—in sandlots—and formed groups and worked our their own rules. Now we've intervened as adults by saying, "No, no, no, we'll work out the rules for you. As a result you don't have to go to very many Little League games to see parents out in the middle of the diamond beating each other up or wanting to kill the ump because of a bad call. Parents are out there in the middle of the playing field screaming at each other, screaming at the kids, "Why didn't you win?" as if the child didn't want to win.
>
> Personal Interview
> **Chuck Hogan**
> Performance Specialist

Carl Jung spoke of the child living in the unconscious of the parent. The parent's implicit beliefs and expectations are decisive factors in the formation of the child's world-self views, even when not spoken or expressed (by the parent) in any way.
Evolution's End

When we moved in on that play period, the sandlot baseball and football, and organized the activity for children, we upset the entire process and destroyed the purpose. If allowed, children will spontaneously get together, form sides, create their own rules and regulations, and compete. Only by forming rules can they have a game. Working out their own rules and calling their own fouls are the critical factors. When adults step in, as we have for the past fifty years with Little League enforce our adult rules and regulations, and set up teams, we steal from children the experience of creating self-regulated social organizations.

Little League

Little League has not given us happy, well-adjusted children. We have all seen parents and coaches at Little League games, shouting at seven- and eight-year-olds who stand heads down as the coach calls them imbeciles and urges them to get out there and really put their all into it. The faces of the little children describe their confusion, guilt, and shame. And the parents are there, lining up on the side of the coach. The children have failed to measure up to the expectations and standards of their parents and coach, who are condemning them publicly. And the children do not even know what for. This is a strange form of modeling, very far indeed from what we know of optimum states of learning and performance.

Washington Post columnist Sally Jenkins, and thousands of other concerned adults see Little League for what it truly is: another adult agenda, not at all child's play. In her column, *Let the Little Kids Play—Without The League*, Sally describes how the Little League World Series was turned upside down recently when it was discovered that the star pitcher was fourteen years old, not twelve.

> The original idea of Little League was merely to help the players do that thing children haven't yet learned to do, organize, and through organization, learn a few simple skills and values. "Character, Courage, Loyalty," says the Little League motto. But let's review the events of the most recent Little League World Series and the values displayed.
>
> The Rolando Paulino All-Stars, nicknamed the Baby Bombers, became a sensation when Almonte threw the first perfect game in the tournament in 44 years and led his team to a 4-1 record and third place. But jealous parents began talking of rumored violations, and two suspicious adult coaches for New York area teams even hired private investigators — private investigators! — to look into Almonte and the Bombers. Next, acting on the rumors, Sports Illustrated — Sports Illustrated! — sent a reporter to the Dominican Republic and uncovered a document suggesting Almonte was really 14. Finally, Dominican officials yesterday determined that Almonte was playing under a false birth certificate obtained by his father, Felipe, who, it seems, is also here with his son illegally, since their visas have expired. Further investigation by the New York Daily News showed Danny was not enrolled in any school in New York. Nor was another player on the team, catcher Francisco Pena,

Insidiously, Little League targeted younger and younger children, until even little tots were dutifully marching out in full advertising array to do battle with the enemy. Whatever might have been left of play after television was killed by Little League and other organized sports leagues, substituting deadly serious adult forms of win-or-lose competition for what had been true play. Gone are the invaluable social learnings, self-restraint, and the ability to decide.

Evolution's End

son of former major leaguer Tony Pena. Which makes it look like the swell little Bronx fairy tale team was more like a nifty little shuttle service from the Dominican Republic for future major leaguers…

What's more twisted? That an ambitious father doctored documents in the hope his son could pitch his way off the island and be noticed by major league scouts, or that adults hired private investigators to check birth certificates?…

Little League should be abolished for the simple reason that children and adults should stay out of each other's circumferences when it comes to games. There should be a decent interval between the crib and the grim business of high school sports, at least one form of play in this world that is not managed by grownups to the point of corruption. What happens when adults manage the games of children is that they manage them the way they manage the rest of their lives—with strife and greed.

Washington Post, September 1, 2001

Our emotional brain is the seat of all relationship. We learn by relating something unknown to something we know. Equally, the emotional brain is the seat of, or at least involved in, memory, recalling what we know. Even the abstract capacity for associative thinking, whether scientific, mathematical, philosophical, logical, whatever, though dependent on our third brain, has its foundation in the feeling state of this old-mammalian brain.
(Antonio Damasio explored this in his book, Descartes' Error.)
The Biology Of Transcendence

Optimum Learning Relationships unfold spontaneously when we feel safe, when we love what we are doing and learn from the experience (all intrinsic motivators). The moment an outside authority steps in and judges the experience, as is the case with all adult-organized athletic programs for children, the instant we introduce rewards and offer praise, approval, or disapproval, the Zone disappears. Learning occurs as it always will, but the lessons learned are not the Character, Courage, and Loyalty advertised by the promoters of the event. Children learn what it takes to win in a contest culture.

Winning & Losing

Authentic play and competition are very different states. One involves a score: the other does not. A score is just a score, a measurement, neither good nor bad. Confusion occurs when we identify with the score, build an image upon it. It is the image that interferes with learning and performance, not the score.

We hear over the loudspeaker Saturday morning: "Will the preschool league please meet on the midget field and the kindergarteners meet over on field number two." We've taken that original playtime and organized it into zero-sum games with winners and losers.

Failure to develop our highest brain lies most often with failure to develop its foundation, the two animal brains. This leads to a circular breakdown of the mirroring dynamics. We can modulate the lower instinctual reactions of our survival-system through our high brain. But our high brain can be developed only on the firm foundations of a well developed survival brain. If we fail to develop the lower, primary brains sufficiently, the higher brain is compromised and can't develop fully. Then the higher can't integrate the lower into its service and so modulate the behaviors of the lower. And when those ancient survival behaviors act without the modification, modulating, or tempering by the higher, trouble brews for that individual, as well as his or her society, and larger body of the living earth.

The Biology of Transcendence

The culture's so focused on the winning and losing. There's this great sucking sound, competition you know, that's going to help kids get a head start. So we teach kids how to compete. They know how to cooperate but they have to be taught how to compete, and guess what they forget to do? They forget about the cooperation.

Personal Interview
Bowen White, MD
Author, Educator, Clown

Right and wrong, win or lose is not part of nature's scheme. Taking a highly stylized, rigid form of action, in which victory is everything and censure plays a heavy role, in which error dogs the child at every breath, and expecting that activity to make the child part of a social team is ridiculous. Competition is inappropriate during early stages of development. Children will never play in that fashion on their own. Competition is not play. Organized competition crops up around age eleven as a prepubescent form of activity. Before that age, children will participate in group activity, but it won't be competitive. Competitive activity is an integral part of natural selection that begins to express through sexuality. At this age children can not be kept from grouping together in some form of competitive activity, nor should they.

Playing in a contest culture ceases to be play. Attention shifts from the joy of learning to short-term results. Results are the consequences of learning, not the goal. When we place results before learning, learning becomes defensive, narrowly focused. We do only what is necessary to win approval, to pass the grade, to win the game. Winning is the highest form of security in a contest culture. Focusing on the score is aggressive.

My high school football practices were more violent than our games because we were killing each other to make the starting lineup—wiping each other out. Wait a minute, isn't this supposed to be a team? We're only a team when there's an opposing team. A team of Little League players is a team only vis-a-vis another team. If that other team is not present, what you've got is inter-team contest and that is as aggressive and hurtful emotionally and physically as the game against another team.

There was an article in the *Times* about the women's Olympic crew. They do fine against another crew. Take that away and they beat each other up. We don't really know what it is to feel real togetherness… The contest culture is designed to keep you on edge, always wondering whether you're in or out. The moment you're on edge your whole physiological system and entire immune system are not working at their highest levels. The whole thing is designed to work against itself.

Personal Interview
O. Fred Donaldson, Ph.D.
Author: <u>Playing by Heart</u>

The system is designed to create winners. That's what competition does. But competition results in many more losers than it does winners. Figure it out mathematically. How many people can get on an NBA team, or an NFL team? All those who don't make it are losers. Listen to football players. Nothing makes any difference unless they win the Super Bowl. A lot of people drop out because it's so aggressive.

Personal Interview
George Leonard
Former Editor, <u>Look Magazine</u>
Author: <u>Mastery, Education & Ecstasy</u>

Magical Parents – Magical Athletes

Concern over the score begins with adults, not with children. The pressure to perform in school is an adult concern, not the child's. Are parents to blame for being concerned over their children's future success? Children need boundaries. The world is dangerous. Children do need discipline. Most adults assume that the pressure they place on their children to conform, to knuckle under and "do it right" is "for their own good." Head Start, the name for our nation's early literacy program, describes the race we are all running. What is a head start? It's getting a jump on the competition.

Do the seventeen "no's" to each "yes" have the desired effect? Does intimidation and control transform the average child into an elite athlete or prima ballerina? How were those who did manage to make it to the top parented, coached, and mentored? What can we learn from the parents and players who did succeed despite all the pressures to remain mediocre?

Yes, most people are driven to be ordinary. Culture strives for that which is common, average. It thrives on ordinary. Our top Olympic distance runners are mediocre compared to the Tarahumara Indians who run 75 to 150

Without that safe place to stand, no energy can be utilized to explore possibility, intent cannot move into content and know fulfillment, the stress of the unknown-unpredictable becomes a chronic threat.
We then spend our lives trying to avoid this threat.
Magical Child

The character, nature and quality of the model environment determines, to an indeterminable degree, the character, nature and quality of the intelligence unfolding in the child. That a French-speaking mamma has a French-speaking child holds with all intelligences. Kittens brought up in an artificial environment of vertical stripes can't perceive horizontal forms later, nor can they learn to. They will stumble into any horizontal object. We humans are more flexible than kittens but still subject to the same model-imperative; the same structural coupling between mind and environment takes place. Our universe will be as big as the stimulus universe provided us initially, our range of participation as wide as our awareness of the dynamics involved.

Evolution's End

miles a day kicking a little ball all the way. Extraordinary depends on what a culture considers normal.

Our goal is to take the lid off learning and performance so we and our children can become the miracles nature intended, in all aspects of our lives. We talked to over thirty world-class golfers and asked them how this could be done. Here is what some had to say.

I had tremendous self-esteem because of my father. It was always "Champ, nice going, champ." If I hit it bad, "Let's see what you can do on the next one." He was never dwelling on the negative. It was always, always dwelling on the positive. Always positive. I had a very secure childhood. I knew he loved me and accepted me. He instilled in me that there's no affirmation stronger than a father's affirmation that you're going to succeed.

Personal Interview
Johnny Miller
PGA Hall of Fame

My dad played golf and I learned to find a peace on the golf course at a young age and I think that's what has helped me to do as well as I have because I don't let things bother me out there. My dad always said it's only a game and you want to enjoy it.

Personal Interview
Nancy Lopez
LPGA Hall of Fame

My dad was great at teaching me to learn from my mistakes and pick the good out of any round, no matter what it was. If I was ten years old and shot 95, he'd say, "but on #4 you hit two beautiful shots and on #16 you hit two beautiful shots, and if we can just get you to do that a couple more times a round..." All the way up to when I was winning tournaments he would say, "All right, you were two or three swings away that day from playing about as good as anybody can play the game." He was always positive. He would ferret out the positive, show it to me, and then show me how to fix what didn't work.

Personal Interview
Davis Love III
PGA Champion

My dad had a refreshingly simple way of looking at the game. The object is to get the ball in the hole. If the ball isn't going in the hole, you're either aiming at the wrong spot or you are mis-hitting the ball. So as I started to play the game, I became immensely curious about how to play it better and how to take strokes off my game. How can I do it better? Nothing related to score, competition, who I was beating, whether I could win a junior trophy or a college scholarship, the PGA tour event, none of that had anything to do with my love for the game. It was all driven by curiosity.

Personal Interview
Mike Reid
PGA Tour Professional

The successful parent is one whose child matures to walk away without a backward glance. Backward glances, either of obsessive love or hatred, show incomplete development, looking back to pick up some missing peaces, to try and patch a broken system.
Bond of Power

Slip into the Zone and championship performance flows naturally. Extraordinary just *happens* in optimum "states," like breathing: without effort or control. If we assume that performance or results are somehow separate from our "state," right here, right now, we miss the most important factor, which is the quality of our relationship to the challenge before us. Performance is a movement of relationship. That is the basic idea. Look again at the "quality of relationship" described by our world-class athletes.

Feeling Safe, Unconditionally Accepted and Loved...
I knew he loved me and accepted me. He instilled in me that there's no affirmation stronger than a father's affirmation that you're going to succeed. It was always "champ, nice going champ." I found peace on the golf course at a young age. They let me play when I wanted to play. Nothing was related to the score.

Play as Learning...
Driven by curiosity. Refreshingly simple, the object is to get the ball in the hole. I learned how to pick the good out of any round, no matter what it was.

Love of the Experience, Intrinsic Motivation...
It's only a game and you want to enjoy it. That gave me my own self-pride, my own self-discipline.

For years Bruce Lipton and other enlightened biologists have observed that environment influences genetic coding every bit as much as conventionally recognized hereditary factors. Lipton found that from the simplest cell on up, a new life unfolds in one of two ways: it can either defend itself against a hostile environment, or open, expand and embrace its world. It can't do both, and environment is the final determinant in the decision made.
The Biology of Transcendence

Watching with Wonder

Formulas and rules may serve as a guide, but no more than that. We respond to our children and the world the best we can, and then we watch with wonder. We watch and learn from our gesture, be it the fly of a ball or a look on our child's face. The looking is the learning. Each moment becomes a learning moment. How the world responds to our behavior is *feedback*. Did the ball go in the hole? If not, we adapt; learn and hit the ball again.

If you think playing championship golf or soccer is challenging, try being a parent. Children are infinitely more intelligent and unpredictable than balls. Imagine how parenting would change if we "played parenting" as carefully as some "play golf." Consider how we observe the fly of the ball, its position on the green, the slope, and distance from the cup. We select just the right club (which is a whole different matter); we ponder and approach the ball with such care. We take a practice swing or two and position ourselves just so. How many people give this quality of attention to their children, to their partners, and to nature? What if the ball had a mind of its own? What if it moved when it wanted, had likes and dislikes, preferred this green to that and communicated these preferences by laughing or crying? If you think golf or tennis is tough, try being a parent.

We asked Chuck Hogan, considered to be a coach's coach, how instruction would change if we were play-based, rather than focusing on the score.

> If we can't have fun, children aren't going to have fun. If we're bored, they'll be bored. If we've got to win to prove we're having fun, they'll have to win to prove they're having fun. The question isn't "what do the kids need to do?" "What do we need to do?—that's the real question." Is it fun or do we have to win to have fun?
>
> On the average we get a whole lot of "no, no, no, no," about 17 to 1 on the no-to-yes ratio. Let's reverse that. What if we simply affirmed the positive and let the negative feedback take care of itself? It would sound something like this:
>
> "All right, you do your stance, Yippy-Skippy, yes, you did it! Way to go! You did it!" "I did?" "YES, you did!" Very quickly the brain gets the idea, Wow! This is kind of fun. This takes a lot of heat off. This is a pretty safe place to be.

Interaction (relationship) is play, but action and reactions are work. The biological plan is aborted when we invert this genetic plan for learning. That is, to approach learning consciously, we think we or the child must do the work of learning, but that is a biological impossibility. The greatest learning that ever takes place in the human mind, a learning of such vastness, such reach, such complexity that it overshadows all other learning, takes place in the first three years of life without the child ever being aware of learning at all.
Magical Child

Now it's time to take a swing at the ball. They swing and miss. Hey, that's okay. That's just fine. It was a perfect example of swinging right over the top of the ball. No problem there. Let's take another swing and see if we can adjust that experience. Now the ball gets hit. Way to go. That's great. That's wonderful. Huh?? Yes, that's wonderful.

Well aren't you going to show me what I'm doing wrong? Why would I show you what you're doing wrong? Whatever you offer the brain is what you're going to get out of the brain. Let's pay attention to what you're doing right, not only at a cerebral, analytical level, but emotionally. Why don't we just go Wahoo!!, until you find out that it's okay to feel that way.

Pretty soon you'll get up in the morning and your brain will automatically say Yippy-Skippy. Let's go throw the ball, kick the ball, hit the ball. I can't come in for dinner mom I'm having too much fun. That's the way we would do it. It's got to be fun.

Personal Interview
Chuck Hogan
Performance Specialist

The Coach

Parenting, like childhood, is a process. It unfolds. It develops. Parenting is relationship. Relationship is learning. Learning is play. Intelligent parenting is playful parenting. The same is true of our coaches. Coaches are role models. Are they controlling children through rewards and punishments or are they evoking and eliciting optimum learning and performance from the inside out?

Great coaches love to coach. They love to interact. They love to play and they don't ever want to stop playing. Good parents can still play but their means of play might have been in business or being a mom. But the key is not to lose that fun, that light, that happiness, that joy of your life in whatever the activity is. To be an example, it first has to be in our lives. And then a good coach, a good parent, fuses that experience, that joy into every aspect of their child's life.

Personal Interview
John Douillard
Author, *Body, Mind and Sport*

That our children become who we are, more or less, rather than what we tell them to be, is a fact that can enrage us. But the Model Imperative is not a cultural invention subject to culture's modifications, it just functions, like gravity. We have ignored for half a century or more the studies that show some 95% of all a child's learning, or "structures of knowledge," form automatically, in direct response to interactions with the environment, while only about 5% form as a result of our verbal "teaching" or intellectual instruction.

The Biology of Transcendence

Relationship is the key ... The infant in the womb has a symbiotic relationship with the mother's body, but this is a limited relationship. Only through separation from this matrix can a larger matrix be explored...

Nature provides that each division, separation, and addition in child development takes place in proper sequence. If nature is violated, overall maturation must fail. For instance, should the child be separated from egocentricity too soon by enforced premature autonomy, or a premature academic schooling, maturation will falter and the child will remain largely in a sensory–motor stage of development (where the bulk of our populace remains)...

If individuation ends in isolation, instead of autonomy there is anxiety; instead of creativity a clinging to matter as matrix; a fear of change and inability for creative abstract thought.

Bond of Power

Keep out of the way, that's the best thing a coach or instructor can do—just allow the learner to do what he or she is going to do. And once in a while - you're there. Some of the greatest lessons I've ever seen were when a word or two made huge changes. We have computers that read out milliseconds of weight transfers. Give a person a different thought, you'll see them change immediately, but start to get into mechanical data and it won't change the person at all.

Personal Interview

Randy Henry

Founder, Henry-Griffith Golf Clubs

The real challenge for a coach, which is no different from the challenge we have in education or in business, is to help young people, adults, and parents see through the invented meanings that have been attributed to winning and losing. And then to create with the individual a meaning that makes more sense, a meaning that will still allow them to benefit from the activity without getting involved in the great false hopes and false failures. Those who do this not only stand to enjoy their job much more, but will bring a dignity to the profession that doesn't exist.

Personal Interview

Tim Gallwey

Author, <u>*The Inner Game*</u>

Expanding Our Boundaries

The potential connections and information exchanges pulsing between the neurons in our brain and body are immeasurable. Most human beings barely scratch the surface. Something is holding us back. There is a great weight, a powerful field called "belief" holding us hostage, compelling us to behave in predetermined patterns. For years it was thought that human beings could not run a mile in less that four minutes. Roger Bannister broke the myth. Optimum Learning Relationships do for parenting and for education what Bannister did for runners. It expands the boundaries, opens the door to new patterns and possibilities.

Sports and athletics is one environment which offers a view of supreme examples of the human system in the "zone" and also examples of evolution on a compressed, accelerating and observable stage for everyone to witness. Bannister's mile, thought to be so stunning and abnormal at the time is now mundane. Breaking records is not exceptional, it is expected. Professional golfers shoot 59, dunking a basketball is ho-hum and 960 on a snowboard is done regularly (if you don't know what a 960 is then you simply are not paying attention).Today's X-games make the Roger Bannister or Wilma Rudolf records look rather pale.

We all have the greatness of the athlete built into every cell of our body. What is very, very interesting is that all of these record-breaking athletes will tell you that their best and most supreme performance was "easy". The challenge was in the preparation. The actually doing "in the zone" required but very little energy from the brain. This is documented by EEG and MRI readings of brain wave activity and topography. In the most literal sense, child's play is where the best happens. John Jerome concludes his book *Sweet Spot In Time* (Sweet Spot being his name for the 'zone') by saying: "About the only thing that can be concluded from all the scientific study of extraordinary performance is that the harder we push the cell the more it will respond. There seems to be no end."

Personal Interview
Chuck Hogan
Performance Specialists

Enculturation; parenting, education, the myths, rituals, beliefs, ideologies, customs and their associated behaviors, create our boundaries. The weight of tradition and today the pull of mass-media marketing prevent all but a very few from reaching beyond tightly prescribed limits. The web is both intensifying and narrowing.

A long-term German study has shown that overall sensitivity to environmental signals has dropped one-percent each year. Thirty years represents a thirty percent decrease in environmental signals reaching our awareness. Subtle impressions simply do not make the cut. The intensity of environmental stimulation is going up while our capacity to experience subtle sensations is going down. Our experience is being homogenized, controlled, shunted into predetermined grooves, and we can not even see it happening. Everything looks so normal. So intense. At home, in the movies and at school.

The U. S. Congress recently approved sweeping educational reforms clearing the way for "high stakes" uniform testing at all grade levels. The

Phenomena have appeared over the past fifty years that have no historical precedent, for which our genetic system can't compensate, and that have so altered our mental makeup that we are blinded to the obvious relation between cause and effect... hospital childbirth, day care, television, and the erosion of child play. Schooling contributes its share and will continue to do so since vested interests view the shambles only as economic or political opportunity. No national "solution" yet forthcoming has moved beyond a politically motivated or "financially viable" position. The massive thrust for computerized education, capturing the public fancy by design, is a case in point. A computer on every desk, software for the millions and billions for the investor, will be the final straw in damaging children beyond all educability. Evolution's End

ideal is to standardize the national education system under a "master plan." The goal is to ensure that each child, in each classroom, is turning the same page in his or her book on the same day throughout the land. Why? So we can compete in the so-called global economy. Or so they say.

Transforming Ourselves First, Then Culture

Our Brave New Industrial Mind

The greater the rate of change the more intense our pressure to predict and control. Today everything is heating up, the planet, the stress we feel, the number of decisions we face every day, the conflicts, and the violence.

It took thousands of years dreaming of flight before the Wright Brothers succeed at Kitty Hawk. Less than seventy years later we landed on the moon. In 1900 the majority of people, 97 percent, lived in rural communities, supported by extended families. Our great-grandparents grew their own food and participated in local, bio-regional, economies. In recent decades the family has been blown apart. Fifty-percent of marriages end in divorce. When asked to draw carrots, New York City preschoolers drew tiny orange squares. American children can recognize only a few plants but easily identify over one hundred corporate logos. "Corporate time," sponsored commercial media, has replaced family time and the bedtime story. Stay-at-home mothering is disappearing as fast as many endangered species. Huge assumptions are driving the rapidly changing world we live in, assumptions that translate directly into parenting and education. Behind the unprecedented changes lurks what ecologist David Orr calls the *industrial mind*.

> Much of the current debate about educational standards and reforms is driven by the belief that we must prepare the young only to compete effectively in the global economy… The kind of discipline-centric education that enabled us to industrialize the earth will not necessarily help heal the damage caused by industrialization. Ultimately the ecological crisis (and the crisis facing childhood) concerns how we think and the institutions that purport to shape and refine the capacity to think… More of the same kind of education will only compound our problems…

> Today we will lose 116 square miles of rain forests, about an acre a second… By year's end the total loss of rain forest will equal an

Why, with a history so rich in noble ideals and lofty philosophies, do we exhibit such abominable behaviors? Our violence toward ourselves and planet is an issue that overshadows and makes a mockery of all our high aspirations… Why, after thousands of years of meditation, has human nature not changed one iota?… Why, after two thousand years of Bible quoting, proselytizing, praying, hymn singing, cathedral building, witch burning, missionaries and canon, has Western civilization but grown more violent and grisly efficient in mass murder? In exploring the issue of transcendence, we explore the issue of our violence by default. The two are intertwined.
The Biology of Transcendence

area the size of Washington state; expanding deserts will equal the size of West Virginia; population will have risen by more than 90,000,000. By the year 2000 perhaps 20 percent of the life forms existent on the planet in the year 1900 will be extinct.

The impact of our industrial mind on the environment is also being reflected in our families, our neighborhoods, and our schools. Child abuse and neglect doubled in America between 1983 and 1996. The number of seriously injured children quadrupled. One million children run away each year. Eighteen million children spend more time in day=care than with their parents. Mothers are the fastest growing segment of the work force. This year over twenty-million prescriptions for highly addictive stimulants will be offered to children to control their behavior, beginning in preschool. Suicide is the third leading cause of death for American children, resulting in a teen attempting suicide every seventy-eight seconds. David Orr continues:

> This is not the work of ignorant people. Rather it is the result of people with BA's, B.S.'s, M.B.A.'s and Ph.Ds. Education, in other words, can be a dangerous thing...*It's not education, but education of a certain kind that will save us...* Educators must become students of the ecologically proficient mind and of the things that must be done to foster such minds. In time this will mean nothing less than the redesign of education itself.
>
> David W. Orr, Ph.D.
Chair of Environmental Studies, Oberlin College
Selected quotes from <u>Earth in Mind, On Education, Environment,
and the Human Prospect</u>

Optimum Learning Relationships open the door to this complete redesign of education and what we call parenting. The shift of state *is* the factor that will reveal new definitions for both.

Each of us and our economic, social, and educational institutions have been shaped by the "industrial mind." We are inside it. As water is transparent to fish, the assumptions and values implicit in our industrial mind are transparent to us. We rarely catch a glimpse of the limitations and deep conditioning that defines our world view. What we do see is the impact our minds have on our families, our children, and the environment.

Bohm, Einstein and others have pointed out that the problems created by the industrial mind can not be solved by that mind. We can not solve a problem at the level of the problem, for the mind that created the problem

For the culturally fragmented person, any move toward wholeness is interpreted as a threat, a final fragmentation, a loss of coherence. When the instrument of the body-brain becomes self-generative, anything not available to its weak energy must be interpreted as destructive. Thus our personal concepts become inverted, we see things backward, and turn heaven into hell.
We have only to let, to allow, and stop gripping. Not because of some divine decree or moral imperative, but simply because of the mechanics of energy and the nature of our mind and brain.
Bond of Power

is the problem. So it is with our current approch to parenting and education. Adults need a new mind, a fresh mind, an original and authentic mind to see beyond the limitations causing so many conflicts in ourselves, our children and the world. Exploring Optimum Learning Relationships opens the door and invites this new mind to meet and respond to the world. And what it reveals will be a revelation to our industrial mind.

Our great challenge, according to Bohm, is to find ways of reaching beyond the pressures and limits imposed by our conditioning. To do this we must discover new states and unfold new capacities that are not confined to our predetermined patterns. Every time we "think" we have arrived, we must return to the optimum state of authentic play and invite the perception of new patterns and possibilities. Rest too long on this belief or that conclusion and we lose the living vitality and intelligence of our true nature.

Many potentials are missed through failure of response from parents, who were in turn not developed in those potentials by their parents, and so on in infinite regress. Every capacity conceivable to imagination is inborn in us, since ours is an open-ended mind/brain, but any specific capacity must be brought forth and developed.
Bond of Power

Optimum Learning Relationships expand the current model of parenting and education by incorporating states of being and relationship as fundamental and increasingly critical components of learning, wellness, and performances at any age, in any field.

Is it practical? Will it achieve the results we are now trying to achieve with our control strategies, our punishments and rewards? A few educators have been experimenting with Optimum Learning Relationships in their classrooms. They found that optimum states:

- Reduced violence, social isolation, and defensive aggression implicit in the contest behaviors of children and adults.

- Increased empathy, cooperation, and perception of community by reducing conflicts normally associated with categories, judgments, and differences.

- Self-esteem, communication skills, and true creativity increased by reducing fears and stress found in most learning environments.

- Increased recognition that touch and movement are essential elements in normal learning and healthy development.

- Students became more complete learners. They became more focused as they felt safer. They learned from the world around them and not just from their teachers. They became more sensitive to observation and change.

- OLR/Play shows us that it is possible to connect with people and other forms of life, both cross-cultural and cross-species.

- OLR/Play continually opens new possibilities.

- There are the positive effects of moving your body through space, learning to read body language, learning about cause-and-effect relationships, learning nonverbal communication skills, learning to pay attention, to focus; to be present in a situation.

- While playing with autistic children, eye contact increased, touch increased, verbalizations increased, social interactions increased, violence decreased, giggling increased. Following play, students were more focused and more willing to attend to other tasks.

- OLR/Play provides a greater opportunity for social skill development. Many of the children that we play with are withdrawn, quiet, and very timid. Play helps to bring children "out of their shell."

By reducing conflicts Optimum Learning Relationships reduce violence and increase safety:

- Students become less violent and are able to work out differences more readily. They are more sensitive to each other and staff.

- They develop strong bonds and feel comfortable throwing an arm around one another without fear of being teased for demonstrating affection.

- They are safer knowing what safe touch is. They know what it feels like to be touched in a positive way so when someone touches them in anger or sexually they readily read the signals.

- They develop an innate sense of "belonging" to the bigger picture.

- Peer pressure is reduced. They don't need to find their sense of "belonging" in their peers or with drugs.

- Play provides a safe space to be who you are and grow (experiential learning). Children learn that "acting out" is

Teilhard de Chardin projects his longing onto a great Omega-Point "out there." But even there we would find some super shell, and we would itch to find its crack. In a peculiarly prophetic vision a century and a half ago, Walt Whitman asked, looking up at the vast universe of stars: "When we have encompassed all those orbs, and know the joys and pleasures of them, will we be satisfied then?" No, he realized, "We but level that lift to rise and go beyond." ...It is time to see man in his true perspective, as Whitman did when he wrote; "... in the faces of men and women I see God, and in my own face in the glass, I find letters from God dropt in the street, and every one is sign'd by God's name."
Crack in the Cosmic Egg

unnecessary in an atmosphere of safety, trust and love.

- Play provides an environment, role modeling, and a definitive design where gentleness is the norm rather than the exception.

And this is just the beginning. We really don't know the limits of human perception, learning, performance. We have never grown up in environments that optimize these potentials. That is, until now.

Part Two

Principles for
Optimum Learning & Peak Performance

Introduction

If play is the optimum state for learning, performance, and well-being, the essence of education, coaching, and parenting, if we expect optimum results, we adults should play—or at least be playful. But alas, playful parenting and education are hardly the norm. Adults have agendas. Is the infant's or child's behavior matching the spoken or nonverbal expectations hidden in the adult agenda? If the child's behavior matches or conforms to the adult's ideal, the child is usually praised or rewarded. If the child's behavior does not match the adult agenda, the child is made aware of his or her breach of conduct, which usually involves some form of punishment, be it a look, a gesture, a harsh No! Optimum learning is play. What we usually think of as learning, education, coaching, and parenting is most often behavior modification, which is never optimal. How do we move individuals and culture from one paradigm to the other, from conditioning to optimum? This question set the stage for a rich dialogue between Michael Mendizza and Joseph Chilton Pearce one foggy October morning in San Francisco.

Open intelligence and flexible logic combine so that the more we learn through personal experience, the more we can learn; the more phenomena and events with which we interact, the greater our ability for more complex interactions.
Magical Child

M: Is there some way to revolutionize the parent-child relationship? Can we take the lid off the limitations we now—even with the best of intentions—impose on children?

J: Model it. Give them the model of whatever it is. We must become the change we wish to see in others.

M: The assumption is that the joy of the experience while in relationship will carry over and the child will want to develop the activity on his or her own, because it's so much fun. But that doesn't always happen.

J: I remember my son John with his bicycle. There was the sidewalk on Faculty Road. He got his bicycle at age five and took it right out that morning. He didn't ask for any help, and it was one of the bloodiest experiences in a kid's life. He fell repeatedly. He bloodied his knees and his hands, and he would be out there, tears streaming down his face. And he'd get back up on that bicycle. He kept doing it. By the end of the day, he was riding that bicycle. Now, he had seen lots of people riding their bicycles and he damned well was going to ride his bicycle too. Nothing we could ever do would drive a child like that. Not even if their tears were from our beating them to learn.

We had a neighbor who also had a five-year-old. The father had bought him a bicycle, and we heard the two of them outside. It was so horrible that I almost called the authorities. That poor child had to suffer his father's berating him, calling him stupid, too dumb to come in out of the rain. "Whatsa matter; I've told you a dozen times. Here's what you do!" He went on and on, and the boy never did learn to ride a bike.

The activity has to be meaningful to children, for they act out of principle. That's the boy on the American farm. That boy was out there at five in the morning protecting the plants against frost. There was never any question about it. They would starve and the child knew it. The whole family was there. No one was exempt. Children took part automatically. To sit on the sideline would literally be outside of the family bond. They sensed the urgency. Piaget speaks of unquestioned acceptance. I'm convinced that the child senses our ambiguity and hesitancy today and acts accordingly.

Neither our violence nor our transcendence is a moral-ethical matter of religion, but an issue of biology. We contain a built-in predisposition and ability to rise above restriction, incapacity, or limitation, a vital adaptive spirit that we have not yet utilized. Our longing for transcendence arises from our intuitive sensing of this adaptive potential, and our violence arises from our failure to develop it.
The Biology of Transcendence

M: On the farm, there was no doubt; there was never any question.

J: Unquestioned acceptance of the given, and the given is the model imperative. The model is who we are and how we relate to the challenge of the moment. The minute there is doubt—"Are we doing the right thing?"—that instantly radiates throughout the whole environment. We are fragmented. The child picks it up, and you've got mayhem in your classroom.

M: There's memorization, conditioning, practice, and they're very important. But it is limited to a predetermined pattern. What kind of environment or circumstance must we create to allow, nurture, and challenge that child into discovering and expanding his or her vast potential? Do you see the difference? One is fixed. We can reward or punish them to conform to a pattern. But that is not enough to optimize development.

J: Parents in the sixties resented all authority. They weren't going to have any authority or structure. Nature's going to take care of this—total free expression. Many progressive educational systems, Waldorf for example, had trouble with this. They have free expression but within carefully designed boundaries. Again, there are two extremes, the lock-step approach and the hippie approach. Maria Montessori was insistent that children need order and discipline. The three-year-old is compelled to organize everything into neat symmetry. If the chairs in the room are orderly one morning and the next morning they're disorderly, the first thing the child does is put things in order.

M: What do you mean by discipline?

J: I'm using the term discipline in the common sense, which means coercive action to modify behavior. The real meaning of the word discipline is disciple, which meant originally a joyful follower. The disciple joyfully followed the teacher. It's far from that today, but to my way of thinking, that would be ideal.

M: A joyful follower is the essence of your model imperative.

J: Sure. If the model matches what children are ready for at that time, they'll go for it with everything they've got. Learning is the way of transcending their current limitations. This is the essence of the modeling imperative. If the model matches their needs that moment, there's never coercion. They will follow joyfully because it transcends their frustrations at that particular time.

M: On the farm there was no ambiguity. No choice was involved. When we talk about today's children, it's really hard to find anything that compelling. The "real" world is very foreign. Their food supply comes from the refrigerator or it's a "happy meal" at McDonald's. They don't have anything "real." At best our demands appear inconvenient. Doing homework may interrupt a TV program.

The meaning of life for many people, including children, is very abstract. It was my idea that John-Michael "should" learn to play the piano, for his own good. We had a close friend whose life was playing the piano. We asked him to play with John-Michael. They had a blast playing together. When the friend left, John-Michael rarely returned to the keys. I, of course, "lowered the boom," as my father used to say. "Get up there and practice, make something of yourself." That was my agenda, not his. I honestly believed it was a disservice not to "make" him practice. Bonnie said no. If the experience itself is not compelling enough, maybe he just doesn't want to play the piano. Maybe piano isn't part of who he's going to end up being. What about picking up his

Firm boundaries give strength to the bond and clarity to those areas, which are open for exploration. The child clearly registers the parent's power of decision and their confidence in their decision. S/he feels bonded to strength. S/he accepts their boundaries and restrictions without frustration or hesitancy because s/he is geared to take cues from them, and their decisions are in keeping with his/her intent.
Magical Child

room, I argued. Maybe not picking up his room—or running into the street—is the boy's true nature. He'll poke his eye out or cut himself if we let him play with sharp knives. It is my job to protect him from his true nature, or so I thought. Living in environments that lack "real" compelling reasons changes radically a young person's desire to do anything.

J: Hans Gefirst said that the child reads early because he senses that it will win the approval of the parent. It will win acclaim. And where do you get that kind of thing? In a highly illiterate household.

M: Are we saying that spontaneous learning takes place to affirm the bond?

J: Any activity, if it is meaningful to a child, will be learned spontaneously. How do we know what is meaningful to that child? The most important thing is to match the model to the developmental period. If there is a match, the child's innate intelligence will respond to it. The key factor is the adult responding to the environment and to the child in ways that match the developmental needs of the child.

M: For a parent or teacher or coach to recognize what's meaningful to a child, they must become skilled observers.

J: Observation means sight and intuition is a form of "in-sight."

M: The act of true observation is an act of intuition.

J: I am aware of my surroundings sometimes and other times I'm not. If I have an agenda, I find that I am often rehearsing my agenda as I walk in the door. The agenda is the only thing I am aware of. My agenda acts like a filter that changes everything to meet the needs of that agenda. I'm likely to override anything that's actually happening. I often don't even notice what is actually going on around me, because I'm so involved with "my" agenda. Adults are full of agendas, especially parents, teachers and coaches.

M: Having an agenda often means that we are not really seeing the child clearly.

J: Our agendas act like the blinders we might use on a horse.

M: Agendas often take the form of concentration. Our focus be-

When the capacity for abstract creativity and pure thought does not develop properly, the solution is not to try to force earlier and earlier abstract thinking, as we now try to do (with reading readiness). Rather, we must provide for full dimensional interactions with the living earth, without allowing abstract ideas to intercede or obscure, so that a sufficient concrete structure may be built from which abstractions can arise.
Evolution's End

comes narrow, which can be very appropriate at times. But to be that focused on our agenda most of the time is much too narrow. With blinders on most of the time we become myopic. We need to let go of that concentration or that agenda and allow another state of awareness to emerge and use concentration as a tool only when needed. With children it seems we are drilling them all the time.

J: It's a matter of focus. Children, especially early children, are global. Up until seven or eight, and maybe even after that, the early child learns in whole blocks. Their learning is instantaneous, as a block, whole, of the model. The crawler suddenly registers the upright stance. He doesn't see it as a series of moves, but as a finished product.

M: Cellular biologist Bruce Lipton, Ph.D., recently shared some very interesting research on brain waves and how they change as a child's brain develops. You mentioned earlier Montessori's description of the "absorbent mind" of the early child and Jean Piaget's observation that early childhood is defined by an "unquestioned acceptance of the given."

Every learning unfolds in the three stages that constitute the cycle of competence. First, the child goes through a period of roughing in some new ability or knowledge...
Second, a period of filling in the details follows the rough grasp achieved...
Third, there is a period of practice and variation, during which the new ability is repeated over and over again.
Magical Child

Recent studies of developmental brainwave activity reveal that before birth and through the first five years of life, the infant/child's brain is generating primarily delta and theta states of awareness similar to a hypnotic trance (Laibow, 1999). Delta (0.5-4 Hz) is associated with an unconscious, sleep-like state. This accounts for the absorbent nature of the early child's brain and also his or her unquestioned acceptance of the adult model environment.

Between two and six years of age, the child begins to express higher levels of activity characterized as theta (4-8 Hz). Theta activity is the state we often experience in the morning, when half asleep and half awake. Around age six the child begins to express higher alpha levels (8-12 Hz), a state associated with calm consciousness. Beta (12-35 Hz), associated with active or focused concentration and attention, doesn't make its full appearance until age ten or twelve.

My adult agenda of John-Michael's needing to practice the piano, for his own good, is a very abstract ideal being imposed on the dream- or trance-like brain of a five-year-old. The adult and the child are living in completely different realities. Unless the adult recognizes and adapts his or her behavior so as to provide the model environment to match the developmental needs of the child, there is going to be trouble, frustration, conflict and despair.

The adult agenda must first be to relate to the child on a frequency that the child can understand, and then to "play" in that reality, communicate on that frequency. The child is incapable of meeting the adult mind. The parent or teacher or coach must enter into and embody the child's mind, which is the gift and the learning for the adult, rediscovering the childlike mind.

J: We usually don't see what the child needs. We only make demands on the child to meet our adult agenda.

M: Let's assume that this is the rule rather than the exception. What would be the alternative, a more appropriate response?

J: The shift is from the adult's own agenda, the focus on a predetermined result, to where the child is now, and what the child needs, moment by moment, and responding according to the actual needs of the situation. The situation is not just the child. The situation involves the child and the parent, each with their agenda, which may be legitimate. The child has needs. So does the adult. Both sets of needs are legitimate. The challenge always is to find the bridge between those two needs. That's where insight comes in.

M: The child needs to explore all of the wonderful things in the supermarket. And mom's got a party in 45 minutes. Conflict is inevitable. Somebody is going to end up crying. The challenge is to hold each set of needs with equal value. Can we meet the child's need for exploration and the mom's needs too?

J   Does the child exist for the parent or the parent for the child? The parent must exist for the child. If the child is not there, the parent survives. If the parent is not there, the child doesn't. Only the adult has the capacity to embody simultaneously the adult world and that of the child. To meet the child only on adult terms is ridiculous. The adult who stretches beyond the blinders of his or her agenda is transcendent. And stretching to meet the adult world is transcendent for the child. The adult-child relationship, when approached in this way, is a spiritual practice for both.

The child is driven to acquire a complete nonspecific or unconditional knowledge of the world. S/he is designed and equipped to acquire information and experience free of value, meaning, purpose, or utility. Adults tend to value all experience and knowledge according to the cultural ideas about utility or worth. An intelligence cued to look for the worth or utility of information or experience immediately closes or screens out possibilities, looking for what can be utilized. An open intelligence and flexible logic cannot be built in this way, although a facile cleverness that can pass for brilliance, given our culture's anxiety-ridden body of knowledge, might develop.
Magical Child

M: This brings up a very important question. Why do we have children in the first place?

J: Very few children are born into the world as a result of conscious conception, because the parents really want this child.

M: We hear about parents going to extraordinary lengths to have a child. Why this burning desire to have a child? Is the child there for the parent or the parent there for the child?

J: For a lot of parents, having a child represents a form of self-fulfillment. The parent has a need for the child, obviously, and the child has a need for the parent. But is it reciprocal?

M: I have the child to fulfill my need, which translates into my "agenda." My agenda is a bias that shapes the relationship even prior to conception. The reason for having the child is my agenda. Wanting the child to be civilized and to learn what I want him or her to learn is my agenda. If I were actually there to serve the needs of the child, taking my cues from the child, and playfully, creatively moving with that, my response would be fundamentally different, and so too would be the fundamental nature of the relationship. My agenda often prevents me from actually seeing the child.

J: This translates into a sense of responsibility. It is not my responsibility to take my signals from that child. I'm responsible for the child, which again is my agenda. To be truly responsible for that child's well-being we must understand and respond to the needs of the child. Their greatest need is for us to be truly responsible to them, but what does that entail? We think it's our agenda.

M: Alice Miller wrote the book *For Your Own Good*, which describes the violence that takes place any time our agenda blinds us to what is actually taking place, either in us or in the child. We have kids because we have an agenda. We want to be fulfilled. That is our agenda. If we continue with that, for their own good, we force them into playing the piano, which is an extension of our agenda. And we're saying that to be truly responsible means that we adults must shift, or have a radically different agenda, or better yet, no agenda. The tranformative power of "bonding" suddenly enters the picture. You start off fulfilling your own needs, but your overwhelming affection for this new human being tran-

Plato said that if he could determine the music young people listened to, he could determine the shape of society. Harvard's Carol Gilligan spoke of our young girls as "confident at eleven, confused at sixteen." She observed a clarity, purity of mind and strong self-image in the eleven-year-old that was smashed in those intervening years. Millions of dollars are made from this destruction, and the destroyed child becomes the destroying but consuming adult. Evolution' End

scends this. Suddenly your greatest need is to serve the child's needs. The actuality of this new human being suddenly transforms the parent's agenda, and we call this bonding. With the bond comes transformation. If no bond takes place, we are left with only our agenda, with its implicit violence. Or am I way off base?

J: No, it's quite solid.

M: Mom has a need to do her shopping and the baby has his or her needs to learn, which expresses as pure play. If we give up connection to our needs and meet only the needs of the other, we lose balance. We lose integrity. Bonding implies a quality of relationship where the needs of both matter equally.

To say that every child is a potential genius may sound ridiculous and even cruel, but to take the current statistical norms as the standard or natural for the child is far more ridiculous and surely more cruel.
Magical Child

J: David Albert, Ph.D., in his book *And The Skylark Sings With Me* describes his relationship with an incredibly precocious daughter. Albert decides that he will take on the task of keeping up with her, to keep up with her because her needs are so intense, so far-reaching, so extraordinary. He drops all of his other activities. And he discovers that she is constantly stretching him beyond all his limits. Then it dawns on him that this is a reciprocal engagement. She is stretching him in all directions when all he wanted to do was coast on his agenda. He found it to be the biggest challenge of his life. They were in a race, but not against each other. His challenge was to stay just ahead of her. Anything less would be to fail the relationship. Yet, to stay ahead of her required the greatest effort of his life. He said, "You know, getting a Ph.D. was simple compared to staying ahead of a really brilliant child." And the child needs that so desperately. They're constantly sending out this message: Here's what I need. Can you meet it? And in order to meet it we have to drop our agenda and really grow. It's an extraordinary adventure, and it's absolutely reciprocal.

M: The child doesn't have to be brilliant or precocious. Children are inviting us in to grow with them, all the time.

J: Many people would say this doesn't apply to them. But it does. The challenge is always to tune our antenna and take our signals from the child. Moment to moment. You talk about a joyful experience!

M: If we were to describe an Optimum Learning Relationship, this would come close.

J: It's reciprocal, where each is bringing the best out of the other. In *Magical Child* I said that the child would bring out the best in the parent and being a parent was our most profound education. The fruition of human life comes in teaching the next generation. The goal for the child is our taking-off place. Each stage is preparing us for fifteen years down the line and, at the same time, it perfects this stage right now. As we're going through each stage with the child, each stage is preparing us for our next move.

M: One of the first things I wrote defining Touch the Future was that the birth of each new human being is a precious opportunity for growth and fulfillment, for the child and for adults as well. One of Bonnie's great joys was this deep sense of connection. She got to look through the child's eyes and in that glance saw all things new again, this time as an adult.

J: She had to drop her agenda and truly be in the moment.

M: You have to be in the moment to rediscover a caterpillar for the first time, again—what it looks and feels like. Sharing in the child's wonder and curiosity opens our wonder and curiosity. For most adults, wonder and curiosity were replaced by an adult agenda long ago. The bond of affection creates a profound shift. The shift is seeing the child as he or she actually is rather than looking through our agenda. Like the Bible says, unless we become as a little child, we can't enter the kingdom. Participating in the baby's innocence and wonder invites us into the kingdom.

J: In *Magical Child* and *Magical Child Matures*, I said that for the child this moment may be the first stage, but for us it is graduate school II. We experience the very same act, but now from a totally different standpoint. In effect, we are God to the child. We are the father who gives good and perfect gifts, and here is the son or daughter. And through that, we begin to catch a glimpse of what our next stage is about. This is transcendence. Each stage overcomes the limitations of the previous. Now as parents we become the mentor, the guide, the mediator and the model. Parenting should bring us to a higher level of the growth process the child is going through. And with that we really come into our own. It is truly transformative.

Everything is preparatory for something else that is in formation, as day must fade into night and night into day... The progression of matrix shifts is from concreteness towards abstraction, or from purely physical world of the womb, mother, earth, and body to the purely mental world of thought itself. The cycle unfolds according to a genetic time-table that is roughly the same in al cultures.
Magical Child

M: You've often said that the birth of a baby opens up whole new intelligences, certainly within the mother, and if the relationship with the father is sound, it will resonate in him. A baby triggers new sets of possibilities that wouldn't have existed had the baby not been there.

J: This is the critical issue. I'm interested in the spiritual development of the human being, and parenting is, or can be, a spiritual process. Tithing and going to church isn't it. Discovering the next stage in my development, by serving the child, is a tremendous thing.

M: If I'm going to approach this thing called parenting or mentoring or being a teacher with a more intelligent and adaptive agenda, where do I begin?

J: The need, of course, is to approach human development as an infinitely open-ended process. The approach to the infinite is through boundaried stages. The boundary grows greater and greater at each stage, moving toward what? Infinite openness. If one approaches infinite openness too soon, without the boundaried stages, we'll get lost. So the ideal is to approach our infinite nature, our godliness, through very carefully boundaried stages. This is how we achieve the highest levels of human development, which can never be known ahead of time. The needs of the child for a boundaried approach can be known. Where that approach leads can never be known. That must unfold by actually navigating through the stages of life.

M: There are many techniques to arrive at particular behaviors. We can condition and modify, and get people to swing a bat, dance, or sing. We can force people into narrow tracks.

J: We can boundary them.

M: We can get them to perform in certain predictable ways through rewards and punishment, but that maintains the cultural lid we have placed on our development.

J: With our current approach the boundary never expands. It can't expand beyond the culture, and our culture is in a mess.

M: If we continue what we're doing, we will keep the lid on human development. Acting as we do literally prevents us from accessing and developing our limitless potential because we keep imposing, as parents

The body manages, somehow and at all costs, to respond to the conceptual framework induced by the hypnotists. Somehow the materials are found to make real, to realize, the mind's notions. A conceptual demand brings about a change in the ordinary mechanisms of life. The same process can be seen in the firewalker, who reverses or nullifies or bypasses the most extreme cause-effect to be found in life.
Crack In The Cosmic Egg

and as a culture, very strict limitations on ourselves and on our children, and always with the best of intentions.

J: The boundaries we usually place on children are not boundaries, but a straitjacket, and they never expand because the culture itself can't allow the expansion of those boundaries. Our culture is bound within certain ways of thinking that can't transcend its problems. Evolution is a means by which nature creates new ways of thinking and being to overcome the limitations of the present set of narrow boundaries. Evolution's response is to create wider boundaries. We honor that by recognizing the boundaries and by recognizing that we're caught in the certain structure that results in enormous violence, and our children act out that violence. And that violence is about to destroy us. We can't move beyond the place in which we have been stuck for so long without pointing a finger at our cultural conditioning, in which we are all caught up.

M: Using the metaphor of evolution, we might say we're trying to evolve new structures, a new set of boundaries, a wider set that reaches beyond the current parental-teacher model. That's what we're suggesting. Without this truly new approach, we are stuck. We're stagnant. We're in an evolutionary cul-de-sac.

J: Which is not going to go anywhere.

M: Our goal is to see if we can articulate the next jump, or expansion in the boundaries we impose, to evolve another, wider set, a more appropriate set.

J: To move beyond the constraints of this culture at this time, a culture turned so murderous and violent, we must begin by realizing the parents' agenda has been created by the culture, by what we think might work for the child. Our purpose is to shift parents from their presupposed agenda, which simply perpetuates the violence, by actually focusing on the child, to discover and co-create a new agenda that might better meet their needs. We must begin by not knowing.

M: We can't know.

J: We can't know ahead of time.

M: True adaptive parenting begins by not knowing what to do. You

No reasonable parent would feed a toothless, nursing infant great wads of steak, no mater how nourishing that steak might be, for the infant would have no tools for assimilating and accommodating that tough meat. The parents of the magical child know that the nutrients of his/her mind-brain growth follow this same qualification. They know that to force the prelogical child to adopt the stances and attitudes of adult logic (or even the logic of a six-year-old) is specifically damaging.
Magical Child

can't know. If you think you know, you'll maintain the violence.

J: Imposing our fixed agenda on the child is an act of violence.

M: By clinging to our agenda, we tighten the bolts that prevent evolution from moving forward.

J: We have to discover evolution's next step, hand in hand with this new life coming in. It has not been conditioned by the constraints that are causing us to murder each other. The only way we can do that is through intuition or insight, by opening up to the child and taking our cues from the child. That itself is a revolutionary step.

M: The act of true observation and intuition will inevitably lead to new insights, and new insights will lead to new models.

J: I think it was the prophet Isaiah who said that a little child would lead us. Why? Because the child hasn't yet been limited by the same repetitive constraints. If we follow that, make that our total response, support and meet the needs of nature's unfolding agenda, which we can only discover moment by moment, by attending and becoming more aware of the child and responding fully to the signals the child sends out, we can discover our own fulfillment.

M: I'm playing with images of creativity, of not knowing, of being open and receptive to inspiration. This moves us towards authentic play, to be in a state of play, to view parenting as a truly playful, creative process. David Bohm once described the essential activity of science (in our case parenting) as thought, which arises in creative perception, which is expressed through play. Bohm described how this play gives rise to provisional knowledge, which then moves outward into action and returns as fresh perception and knowledge. This involves continuous adaptation, which undergoes constant growth, transformation, and extension. He felt that knowledge, and in our case, parenting, is not something rigid and fixed but is a continual process of change. Its form is closer to that of an organism than to a databank. When serious contradictions are encountered, Bohm believed, it is necessary to return to creative perception and free play, which transform the state of our relationships and what we call knowledge. And here is the key. Knowledge, or parenting, apart from this cycle of continual transformation,

Adults view their world through an elaborate web of propositions inherited from ages past, unconsciously adopted as they grew up, rigorously learned in school, and assumed to be absolutely true and necessary or reality adaptation, survival, and social acceptance. Adults see the world through this complex grid of abstract ideas in much the same way the early child see his or her reality through a web of fantasy.
Magical Child

becomes dangerous.

His use of the word provisional is important. Knowledge, our beliefs, our approach to parenting, the adult agenda must be provisional, not fixed or absolute. An approach that may have worked yesterday may not today. We have to be willing to re-evaluate and constantly update our approach to the child. It's never fixed.

An infant who never experiences restraint, in any form, will never need restraining.
The Biology of Transcendence

J: That's his provisional aspect.

M: Parenting can never be reduced to a formula. The breathtaking implication of Bohm's statement is that knowledge, which translates into our agenda for parenting, for education and coaching—which is not subject to this continual renewal—has no meaning. Parenting is meaning-less or becomes violent unless it's updated as a living process.

J: And for this to take place, adults must be willing to suspend their preconceptions, their agenda. They must be willing to venture into the unknown and play.

Principles for Peak Performance & Optimum Learning

We have never experienced this moment before. Never in our personal history, or the history of the universe has this moment, with its challenges and joys, the sun and moon, the tides and planets, the stars and the wind dancing across the sky, ever been quite like this present moment; and what a miracle this moment is. What a gift it is to be a human being, to experience and explore this moment with all our senses and capacities fully alive, the unique combination of which makes us uniquely human. Do we meet, evaluate, judge, and experience this moment through the filter of the past, through all the ideas and opinions we have collected, our beliefs and knowledge, or do we listen, observe, feel, and respond afresh, without trying to predict and control this magical moment or fit our predetermined patterns?

Most of what we call parenting, most of education and most of coaching is an attempt to reward or punish children into behaving in ways we feel are acceptable; a never-ending process that we adults justify and defend claiming that it is "for their own good." This implies, does it not, that we know what is best for them, that we know how they should and should not act, what they should and should not think and feel. When we observe a child, especially our own child, acting in ways that do not match our "image" of the "right way" to behave, we feel it is our responsibility to correct them. To not do so feels irresponsible.

Just as the particular frequencies picked up by our television receiver determines what we experience on the screen, the wave-fields of frequencies to which our neural structures of the brain are tuned determine the nature of what we perceive as our physical, intellectual, and emotional reality, the reality of our thought and awareness.
Evolution's End

Our normal response to children as parents, educators and coaches, which we experience as necessary, implies, does it not, a form of prejudice, prejudgment. Racism is prejudging a person based on assumptions of color or ethnicity. Parenting very often implies prejudging children in very similar ways. To prejudge means that we have come to conclusions and are responding, not based on what is actual, but rather on past beliefs, assumptions, which may or may not apply to this brand new moment. The greater our conviction that our prejudgments, our prejudices, are "true" and "necessary," the more forcefully we demand compliance. This strict imposition of our adult past on the child's present and future creates its own dynamic, which often implies conflict and resistance. Resistance and conflict diminish the attention and energy we have to meet fully and completely the unique opportunities and challenges of this moment. We refer to this as the adult agenda.

Recall Ashley Montagu's description of the magical qualities we admire most in children:

126

Curiosity is one of the most important; imaginativeness; playfulness; open-mindedness; willingness to experiment; flexibility; humor; energy; receptiveness to new ideas; honesty; eagerness to learn; and perhaps the most pervasive and most valuable of all, the need to love.

Adults fail to understand that those childlike qualities constitute the most valuable possession of our species, to be cherished, nurtured and cultivated [all the days of our lives]. They fail to realize that the child surpasses the adult by the wealth of his possibilities. In a very real sense infants and children implicitly know a great deal more concerning many aspects of growing than adults; adults, therefore, have more to learn from them about such matters than the latter have to learn from adults.

Ashley Montagu
Growing Young, The Genius of Childhood, Recaptured

Our challenge as adults—parents, educators, and coaches—is to integrate these qualities as active components into our "agenda." In addition to and balanced with all the good things we wish to share with our children, for their own good of course, we need to remain inquisitive; imaginative; playful; open-minded; we must be willing to experiment; be flexible; laugh; have energy and passion; be receptive to new ideas; speak the truth; enjoy learning; and love.

None of these qualities involve prejudgments. None are based on "ideas" or involve "knowledge." Playful is a state of being, a quality of relationship. Being imaginative, being flexible, being receptive, being honest, all are states of "being." And these childlike qualities or states are very different from the dictators many of us become when our image of what a "good" child should or should not be is challenged by the behavior of children, especially our own. Imposing on children the wisdom and information we have acquired without these childlike qualities creates a very different relationship than if these qualities are present in the relationship.

We are not, for one moment, denying the need and value of information, wisdom, and mentoring. Far from it. We are suggesting that the nature and quality of the relationship, which involves the presence or absence of these childlike qualities, being expressed in an adult form, alters dramatically what the child learns and remembers of our agenda.

As Montagu makes abundantly clear, the goal of development is to retain these childlike qualities into adulthood, not to abandon them as so many of us have done.

If we started with the infant mind, compared it with each successive stage computing corresponding increases in ability all the way to adulthood, and them computed on like increases beyond, we might gain some indication of the power inherent in us.
Evolution's End

Guidelines

Alan Watts, an original translator of Eastern philosophy, once said: "We can't catch the wind in a paper bag." Translation: life is always moving, growing, changing, disintegrating, creating; and so it is with intelligence, for you and I and our children. Neither life nor intelligence can be reduced to a formula, a fixed predictable pattern, which seems to be the basic goal of parenting and of education. Note the conflict. Knowledge and beliefs become fixed metaphors for the living, dynamic, changing processes we call human beings. Childhood, like life and intelligence, is constantly moving and dynamic. Words and ideas can describe this movement, but the word, the description is not the thing. The description is not the described. The images, ideals and symbols we have created about ourselves and our children are not really we or they. Conflict is sure to follow if we mistake one for the other, or try to constrain the living process to conform to our fixed metaphors. Try as we may, we can not catch the wind in a paper sack.

Multi-Dimensional Human Beings

Just as the particular frequencies picked up by our television receiver determines what we experience on the screen, the wave-fields of frequencies to which our neural structures of the brain are tuned determine the nature of what we perceive as our physical, intellectual, and emotional reality, the reality of our thought and awareness.
Evolution's End

We exist and express multiple realities simultaneously; physical (sensory, material), emotional (cognitive, relational), symbolic (metaphoric, rational), spiritual (the nonmaterial, subtle energies). Each reality, each intelligence, as Howard Gardner described in his theory of multiple intelligences, is "real." The reality Daniel Goleman describes in his book *Emotional Intelligence* is very different from our intellectual, symbolic-metaphoric reality. Each reality system operates and affects its own dimension. Thoughts affect other thoughts; feelings affect other feelings. Thoughts also affect feelings, and feelings can express as thoughts. Each is discrete and each can and does affect other dimensions. These multiple realities are simultaneously expressing, more or less, as perception, or at least each has the potential to do so. One dimension of reality is not superior to the other. Each is "real," and each contributes its unique part of the miraculous complexity we call being human.

Holistic learning and living recognizes, develops and integrates these dimensions and their capacities into coherent, flowing relationships. Thought, feeling, and action are complimentary, interdependent and balanced. One dimension is not in conflict with the others.

Our intent is to open and expand and express multiple dimensions in the adult-child relationship. The active power of each principle is its potential

becomes. The message is astonishingly simple. The younger the child, the more that actual state of the relationship *is* the content of each learning opportunity. Slowly, as the child's body, mind, and emotions develop, so too does the capacity for abstraction. But never do abstract ideas replace the meaning or information being expressed and shared in the relationship. The relationship is a channel of communication through which the abstract is conveyed. As Marshall McLuhan said years ago, the medium *is* the message. Form *is* content. The form in this case is the state of the relationship. The relationship itself is primary *content*, which is learned and remembered.

The ideal, especially for the younger child, is for the actual relationship or activity to embody the abstract without making the abstract the focus of the relationship. A simple example is the goal of teaching a young child mathematical concepts—weight, measurement, fractions. One parent sits the child down with paper and pencil and tries to *explain* the difference between 1/2 and 3/4, as might take place in school, using words to explain abstract ideas. The other parent gets out a cookie sheet and begins mixing ingredients for chocolate chip cookies. At five or six years old, which activity would you in-joy more? I would take chocolate over pencils any time, and so would you. Let's see—two cups of flour, one-half cup butter, one-quarter-cup sugar, three cups of chocolate chips . . . Just kidding. That is one-half cup of chips.

With cookies the relationship embodies the abstract ideas rather than abstract ideas defining the relationship. The relationship models the abstract without making the abstract the goal of the experience. Play on the surface, and learning takes place beneath awareness, automatically, naturally. When you think about it, just about everything a young child or even the middle child needs to learn can be accomplished through play. That is, if the adult is playful.

As we adults free ourselves from the false beliefs and limitations we have accepted about ourselves, we naturally access, become, and model a wider spectrum of capacities. We do not have to "teach" our children this wider state. They will achieve this more expansive, playful state effortlessly by participating in our field. It is the state or quality of relationship they will embody, not necessarily a particular skill. Optimum states provide the optimum environment for skills to unfold. That is the point.

> *Each new stage opens capacities beyond those of the previous stage. Although in retrospect we can see clearly how everything in a previous stage prepares for the next, no period in itself suggests the powers to come.*
> *Evolution's End*

If we are to reach beyond the limitations we impose on ourselves and on our children, the change must begin with the adult, right now, in this present moment. *Being Attentive to Being* encourages this change by leveraging the powerful catalysts of love, care, and hope adults have for children. If we accomplish nothing more than embracing and embodying this first principle, *Being Attentive to Being,* our efforts will be truly revolutionary. We will set in motion a radical change in adults, a change that will instantly resonate throughout the lives of children, society, and the world.

Principle Two
Safe Enough to Play
(Protecting, Belonging, the Safe Place)

Optimum Learning Relationships are psychologically safe. The phrase *unconditional love* describes this complete psychological safety, acceptance, and feeling of belonging. To love others unconditionally one must accept and love oneself unconditionally. Easily said, for most, and very difficult to do. We compare, judge, justify, and defend ourselves and others constantly. The *Zone*, state of *Flow,* and original *Play* exist in those rare moments when we feel *Safe Enough to Play.*

The model imperative implies that adults themselves must feel safe before they can create a safe place for children. How do we, having been raised in what Fred Donaldson calls our "contest culture," find this safe place in ourselves and extend that space to include children? Principle two, *Safe Enough to Play,* addresses this challenge we all face.

Are the demands we make of children threatening in any way? Is a failure to perform at certain levels, or a failure to match our behavioral expectations interpreted by the child as a personal failure? Are disapproval, rejection, a break in the bond, a dented self-image, part of the price he or she must pay for failure? Is one's self image, esteem, and worth based on performance? Is approval of others an integral need/component of our self-image? Or, do we and our children understand very clearly that performance/behavior is one thing and that our fundamental character, essence, spirit, and soul, our worth as human beings, are quite a different matter? It is a rare person indeed who is completely clear about this distinction.

Fred Shoemaker, a golf professional and founder of *Extraordinary Golf,* put it this way:

Nature has designed us so that our development from concreteness to abstraction takes place through a series of shifts from one matrix to another. Matrix is the Latin word for womb. The word designates a threefold condition: a source of possibility; energy to explore that possibility; and a safe place for that exploration to unfold. The womb of the mother is, fittingly enough, the ideal example, it provides a source of possibility for new life; the energy for that possibility to be explored by that new life; and a safe environment for that exploration.
Bond of Power

I played in over three hundred golf tournaments by the time I was twenty-one. I never walked off a golf course and had anyone, other than my parents, ever ask me the really interesting questions. One of those might be, "What kind of human being are you becoming by using sticks and balls?" or "What is the purpose of it all?" I never got those questions. I thought the love I would receive was contingent on what I shot and that my character and my score were somehow related. I have given 41,000 golf lessons and not one person in all those years has ever had that completely separated. At some level everybody knows that they're the same delightful human beings whether they shoot a 41 or a 61. But that's not the feedback most of us get. From the very beginning we are taught to believe that who we are and our performance are intertwined. There's a big myth in that, a big lie.

Personal Interview
Fred Shoemaker
Director of Extraordinary Golf

Our second principle, *Safe Enough to Play,* is perhaps the most important step we can take toward achieving or entering into *Optimum Learning Relationships.* Can I meet this moment completely, with all of my energy and attention, or must I hold back some part of myself to protect myself? Recall cellular biologist Bruce Lipton's description of two distinct "states" of the vascular system: growth and defense. In the growth state, the safe state, there is constant renewal and expansion of potential. When the person is threatened, growth is replaced by protection. One can grow elaborate and complex protective capacities, but only at the expense of other potentials. So it is with all living things and especially new human beings.

If children are not provided a safe space, if they are threatened, damaged or traumatized, they close into a tight defense against the world they cannot trust. This impairs neural development and results in completely different structures of knowledge.

The primary responsibility for parents and caregivers is to protect the child by providing a physically and psychologically safe place for children to grow. This requires, first and foremost, that the relationship with the adult be completely safe. When the source of a child's safety and security (the parent or caregiver) becomes threatening, learning, performance, and wellness collapse.

Safe Enough to Play is the guiding principle. On a purely practical level the Lord's Prayer, one of the most quoted texts in the Bible, offers some simple very advice: "and forgive us our trespasses, as we forgive those who trespass against us." The prejudgments we have about ourselves, others, and our children are trespasses. They encroach on our inherent integrity and self-worth. Applying this simple phrase completely to ourselves and to our children transforms the relationship into one of unconditional love and acceptance. The key is to model this unconditional acceptance in our relationships by distinguishing very clearly between performance and character. The challenge is to find ways to communicate that the performance, behavior, or score that might be improved is not confused with the character or inherent value of the person.

Principle Three
Invite the Unexpected
(Suspending Assumptions)

To discover anything new, one must set aside or suspend the old. Again, this is easily said and often very difficult to do. Why? Because comparing new sensory data with what is known or expected is a primary "associative" function of the brain. It happens automatically, like breathing. This comparison is taking place in the background of awareness all the time, moment by moment. The instant something unfamiliar is registered we go on full alert, a phenomenon called the "startle" effect. We wake up, literally, and give full attention to the alien experience. Who knows, it might be an alien. No time to "think." Survival may be on the line.

Our normal state, however, is not so fully awake. Based on years of experience we "assume" that today will be pretty much like yesterday. We assume that the floor is solid, that our shoes are where we put them, that the school bus will be on time. Our relationship to the world, and just about everything in it, including our children, is based on thousands of assumptions. We are quite comfortable, complacent, and content when the outer world matches our inner assumptions. When it does not, we become anxious and uncomfortable. Things aren't the way they "should" be.

Assumptions are great, especially when related to concrete objects. Rocks and trees are pretty predictable. Dynamic, rapidly changing relationships are less predictable—the wind or weather, for example. The more

Nature never abandons a system that works, but builds new, enlarged and more efficient systems on it. She seems to have added each new evolutionary brain to correct problems in an older system, and/or expand its possibilities. All this we inherit as three neural blueprints that are filled in by the actual content of life's ever-changing environments, thus our extraordinary adaptability.

The striking differences between these three structures make this heritage of ours a blessing and curse, however:

When integrated, these three systems offer us an open-ended potential, an ability to rise and go beyond all constraint or limitation.

When that integration fails, our mind is a house divided against itself, our behavior a paradoxical civil war, and we are our own worst enemy.

The Biology of Translucence

abstract and dynamic the form, the more quickly our assumptions break down.

Intelligence, however, is fluid, dynamic, at times messy, chaotic, unpredictable. Assumptions regarding what should and should not be are, at close examination, only rough guides when dealing with intelligent, dynamic living systems, children for example. Conflict between "what is" and what we assume "should be" is inevitable if our assumptions are absolutely true.

Most assumptions are tacit, however. They are implicit, unspoken. They operate beneath our level of awareness. Of the tens of thousands of assumptions we hold, some are true, but many are not. True or false, we unconsciously treat them all as true. Being reflexive by nature, knee-jerk mechanical responses—assumptions—are most often our first response. For most of human history, survival has depended on this instant response.

Relationships are defined, more or less, by these unconscious patterns. We inherited our personal assumptions from others, from the pool we call culture. Culture expresses as individuals and through their relationships the unique set of assumptions that defines the culture are passed on. Each participates in the process by mirroring the culture's pool of assumptions in his or her relationships. To not do so would render the dissident an outcast, or worse still, a lunatic.

We do not *choose* to act on our assumptions, they happen automatically. Being predetermined patterns, assumptions involve little conscious attention and no true intelligence. This is an important point and worth repeating. Predetermined responses, responses that happen automatically, involve very little or no true intelligence. When we respond to others in this reflexive, prejudged manner, we are behaving mechanically.

Assumptions are not bad. They serve very important functions. Our challenge when dealing with intelligent, dynamic systems is not to be completely dominated and driven by our prejudgments. A space or interval needs to be created between the automatic judgment, "this is right" or "this is wrong," and our response. If we act without this interval, assumptions will dominate our lives and define our relationships.

Assuming that we know *the right way* implies, does it not, that all other ways are wrong. Life is a battle. This is right and this is wrong. If they, meaning everyone else, and especially our own children, would simply do things our way (*my* way, really), the world would be a better place. Much of what we call parenting implies this battle. We, parents, "know" what we

Nature's pattern of development is itself threefold. First: each new structure is built on the foundation of neural structures coming before it. Second: As each new brain develops, it incorporates into its own functions the more primitive foundation on which it is built, and changes the nature of that foundation into a nature compatible with the new system. And third: The new integrated system then serves as foundation to a higher evolutionary development in turn. All of which is transcendence in action.
The Biology of Transcendence

are talking about and "by God" you, the child, had better do as you're told, or else! This is what my father called "lowering the boom." Responding to dynamic, intelligent systems with fixed mechanical assumptions implies conflict, and conflict often involves violence. As life becomes more complex we gather and meet the world with more assumptions.

To *Invite the Unexpected* we must suspend the idea that our assumptions are "the only" or "the right" response. Rather than acting immediately on our expectation that life must conform to our prejudice—*my way is <u>the</u> right way*—we witness these first impressions and treat them not as absolutely true and necessary, but provisionally, as one of many possibilities. Creating an interval between automatically acting on our assumptions and how we actually respond invites something unexpected to intervene, some new pattern or undreamed-of possibilities. *Inviting the Unexpected* creates a new and flexible relationship. Life, and all its relationships, becomes more fluid, more flexible.

Principle Four
Take Your Cues from the Child
(The Art of Listening & Observing)

"Take your cues from the child" (or the environment) is the golden rule for Optimum Learning Relationships. To do so adults must develop deep observing and listening skills. They must become sensitive to the outward expressions a child makes and also to the ever-changing flow of inner states. The art of seeing, hearing and sensing deeply demands a quiet mind, a mind that is alert and sensitive, and a heart that can really love. If we are preoccupied with our agenda, that is what we will see. Rather than seeing, feeling, and understanding who the child is, this moment, we will be, quietly or not, comparing the child's behavior with our preconceptions. We will not see what *is*. We will see only what *should be*.

Meeting children with our fixed assumptions is a betrayal of their and our own true nature. Every few days the child is born again, transformed. Emerging capacities shift his or her reality from the physical to the emotional to the increasingly abstract. In part one we outlined the different ages and stages of child development and what cues may be found for each. These general guides help adults adjust their expectations and expressions to match the developmental needs and capacities of the emerging child. The key is to not impose adult expectations on a child's immature capaci-

The average human brain has some 10 billion neurons, or thinking cells, but intelligence rests not so much on the number of cells, as on the number of connections between these cells. A neuron can have as many as 10,000 connecting links (dendrites and axons), with other cells or almost none. A single cell can be directly linked with as many as 600,000 other cells. These connecting links and the patterns of rhythmic cell firing possible through such linkages are what provide the ability to process information. The more the connecting links, the greater the brain's computational ability.
Magical Child

ties. Two classic and common examples are demanding that preadolescent children participate in professional forms of competitive games, e.g. Little League, and imposing reading and writing on the early child. Both are examples of an adult agenda supplanting the child's natural, biological enfoldment. To maintain the bond and win the approval, children will strive to succeed at the premature challenges we demand and will usually fall short of our expectations. These early failures worm their way deeply in the psyche and become permanent fixtures of the child's emerging self-image. And our premature demands block full development of those capacities that are appropriate to the child's particular age and stage. Partial development of early stages compromises the optimal unfolding of later stages. Personal development stumbles, and with it the evolution of culture and the species.

Taking your cues from the child implies an adult state that is quiet, listening, observing, sensitive, and curious, a state that is not completely committed to or invested in prejudgments. Only such heart and mind can actually perceive, learn from, and respond to "what is." Being in this state, the adult is learning from the relationship as he or she participates in it. The goal is to lift our response out of what David Bohm called the *reflex system*. Reflexes involve little or no intelligence. To invite intelligence into the relationship demands greater energy and attention than defaulting to reflexes. "Taking your cues from the child" implies this added energy, attention, and intelligence. Looking for cues represents a very different quality of attention than assuming we know what should and should not be.

This subtle but radical shift in energy and attention radiates throughout the relationship. The child senses that he or she is actually being seen, really felt and understood. Children trust adults who bring such care and attention to the relationship. They feel respected and express this respect freely. Trust, respect, shared meaning, and creative learning fill the relationship.

To observe in this way is to literally "not know" what the child or we might be the next moment. Prediction and control may have a place in the relationship, but not the only place. Parents, educators, and caregivers find this very challenging; they like being in control. Our invitation is to become again as a young child, to look, feel, and experience the world as if it were for the first time, but from the vantage point of maturity. Taking our cues from the child opens new universes of empathy and understanding. Behold, all things are made new again.

Principle Five
Respond Deeply & Completely
(The Awakening of Intelligence)

Alvin Toffler in his book *Future Shock* warned that the increasing speed at which culture moves will change our lives dramatically. We are busy, occupied, stretched to the limit, stressed, over-committed. Researchers point out that challenges that demand a shift in context are much more stressful that challenges of a like kind. Responding to a three-year-old in the middle of a business call, for example, is more stressful than dealing directly with a business challenge. Responding to the child while in a business mode requires a shift of context. We are challenged from two or more directions at the same moment. Attention splits. Our response to each challenge is compromised; it becomes more superficial, more mechanical, and less optimal.

Responding Deeply & Completely requires two things: undivided attention and space (time, leisure, an interval or gap) between the conditioned reflexive response and the unexpected. If no interval exists, the reflex system takes over. Our response is habitual, mechanical, predetermined.

Our first four principles cultivate and gather attention. We are more aware of our state of being. We feel safe enough to play and extend our "safe place" to include the child. We suspend our agenda and invite the unexpected. We listen, observe, and take our cues from the child rather than superimposing our agenda on the moment. Each of these playful practices demands greater attention, and this increased attention literally transform us and our relationships, that moment. For what, you ask? For a deep and complete response to the world and all its challenges.

Even in the middle of pregnancy if there is a change from negative to positive in the mother's emotional life, the direction in fetal brain growth changes accordingly.
The Biology of Transcendence

Real transformation of ourselves and our relationships unfolds in the response we make to this present moment. The philosopher J. Krishnamurti put it quite simply: "Reincarnate now." In making that statement he challenged two things: the role of knowledge and the role of time in this transformation. By knowledge he meant the reflex system, our conditioning, what we know and assumptions implicit in our knowing. By time he meant "becoming," using the known past to create something completely new. The past can modify itself endlessly. In doing so we have the feeling that we are making progress when in fact we remain bound to the same old patterns.

According to research, our brain works by neural "fields," groups of neurons operation in units. A neuron is a large brain cell that vibrates at a certain frequency and dies if this vibration ceases...

In our neocortex, neurons are organized into fields of a million or so, relating through dendrites and axons. A single adult neuron connects with an average of ten thousand others to form such groups. The resulting networks create various forms of information-experience through exchanges of frequency of "information" between neurons and fields...

Neurons don't contain information any more then the transistors or tubes of a radio contain the shows they play. They "translate" potential frequencies with which they are resonate and to which they have been "tuned" or keyed.

Evolution's End

Unless I fundamentally change, the future will be what I have now. This is a simple fact. If I am vicious, cruel, brutal, today, as I have been in the past, I'll be that tomorrow. You can't get away from it. If I am quarrelling with my wife or husband and so on, I'll do it tomorrow too. So tomorrow is now. And to break this chain in which we are caught, there must be a mutation now.

J. Krishnamurti
Ojai, California, 1985

Years ago Ram Dass (Richard Alpert, Ph.D.) popularized the "eternal present" in *Be Here Now*, claiming that if we give complete attention to the present, the future takes care of itself. More recently Eckhart Tolle described the same idea in his book *The Power of Now*. Creativity, intelligence and insight are not products of habit, of the reflex system. Intelligence is innate, not accumulated or learned and is woven throughout every cell of our body and all of nature. Our challenge is to access this vast intelligence and to meet the moment with both our reflexes and insight-intelligence. It sounds very complicated but in practice it is very easy, so easy in fact that it feels like *Doing Nothing* at all, yet another book on transforming consciousness, by Steven Harrison.

Innate intelligence is always "acting" for our well-being and the well-being of our relationship/environment. The reflex system, knowledge and its assumptions, often blocks and prevents our experiencing this deeper wisdom. Reflexes may be compared to a bully playing loud music on a quiet summer afternoon. The quiet sounds of nature, our nature, the wind in the trees, the birds, the sound of our own innate wisdom are pushed aside by our bully reflexes, insisting that the world conform to our or her agenda, or else. Suspending our agenda, inviting the unexpected, accepts and respects the need for reflexes and simultaneously looks deeper for emerging wisdom and intelligence, which is always new and creative, never "known." Intelligence "acts" spontaneously, naturally without our having to "do" anything at all. By giving space for intelligence to express we discover that reflexes are only one of many possibilities. This opens the door to original or authentic play, as O. Fred Donaldson describes so well.

Deep in our nature is original play, which is far more fundamental than the games and rules we have invented. Original play is both an all-embracing vision of reality and a practice of kindness, which permeates all of one's relationships. To play in this way is to be in touch and to be touched deeply by our authentic human nature and the natural world. Original play cultivates an ever-renewing sense of enchantment and engagement with the world. It develops calmness, awareness and a flexible ability to handle stress, surprise or challenges without aggression. This play develops radically different behaviors than those encouraged by the dominant contest culture. The response is deeper, more universal and authentic. When in this play the limitations of our cultural identity drop away, leaving the dynamic relationship of the two faces of God, exploring, learning together. Original play is truly an ecological intelligence. The sensitivity this play develops needs to be understood and integrated into all aspects of family, community and professional life. Discovering the intelligence of play opens once again the genius of childhood most of us lost long ago.

O. Fred Donaldson, Ph.D.
Essay on Original Play with Michael Mendizza

Responding Deeply & Completely to the child rather than mechanically or superficially resonates throughout the relationship. The deeper adult response challenges the child to respond in kind. New patterns and possibilities emerge that "act" in unexpected and creative ways. Playing with the new and novel becomes feedback and the source for the next insight, challenging and transforming both child and adult. The adult and child provide for each other the exact catalyst needed to transcend the limitations of their current patterns, habits, and reflexes. Each mentors the other in new and novel ways, and each is born again and again through the ever-changing play of their relationship. Is it always this new and creative? Certainly not. But the possibility for some new discovery exists each and every moment and that imminent possibility changes everything.

The great rule is: Play on the surface, and the work takes place beneath... Growth of intelligence is never a conscious process: conceptual changes always take place below awareness.
Magical Child

Principle Six
Imagine
(More on Television & Computers)

Imagination is such an important issue. It demands some exploration of related issues such as language development, the use and abuse of television, clear and creative thinking, computers, higher learning and aggression.

Our previous principle, *Responding Deeply & Completely,* opens the door and invites creative intelligence to express in and through our relationships. This intelligence is ever-present, percolating beneath the surface of awareness. Get out of the way, suspend assumptions and agendas, quiet the mind, and there it is. David Bohm and the philosopher J. Krishnamurti called this vast innate wisdom *insight*. For those who have eyes, let them see.

Another form of creativity, one in which we actively participate, is imagination. Einstein knew that imagination was more important than knowledge. He understood that our greatest discoveries and most profound works of art are created and refined first in the inner world we call imagination. Far from being a waste of time, the daydreams and fantasies of childhood build the foundation for all higher learning. Yet, imagination is rarely developed. The model imperative holds true for imagination as it does for all other capacities. A well-developed adult model and enriched, challenging environment and the child spontaneously, playfully responds. No external model or environmental challenge, no development.

William Blake considered our capacity for imagination to be our "divine genius."
Crack In The Cosmic Egg

The dictionary defines imagination as the ability to create images not present to the sensory system. The environmental challenges or stimuli that evoke these inner images are descriptive words, symbols, and metaphors. Of the many changes impacting childhood one of the most dramatic is early language environment. In 1991 *Newsweek* reported that the typical teen in 1950 B.T. (before television) had a spoken vocabulary of 25,000 different words. Today's teens have vocabularies of 10,000 words, which implies a corresponding reduction in critical and creative thinking skills.

"Sagging Syntax, Sloppy Semantics, and Fuzzy Thinking" begins chapter five of Jane Healy's wonderful book, *Endangered Minds, Why Children Don't Think, and What We Can Do About It.* Healy describes how language skills, verbal and written, organize and define how we think. Rich and varied language skills translate into greater capacity to understand abstract concepts, perceive ratio and relationships, to think critically and creatively; all are byproducts of imagination.

Our cosmic egg is the sum total of our notions of what the world is, notions which define what reality ca!n be for us. The crack, then, is a mode of thinking through which imagination can escape the mundane and create a new cosmic egg.
Crack In The Cosmic Egg

Writing is the road test for language as a vehicle for thought. An alarming number of students coming off our linguistic assembly lines are failing it. "Very few of our students can write well," states Archie E. Lapointe, executive director of the National Assessment of Educational Progress. "Most students, majority and minority alike, are unable to write adequately except in response to the simplest of tasks."

Well-reasoned and well-organized writing proceeds from a mind trained to use words analytically. No matter how good, how creative, or how worthy a student's ideas, their effectiveness is constrained by the language in which they are wrapped... The verbal tools that clarify relationship in reading and writing do the same job in math, and studies of children with exceptional mathematical talents often reveal similarly high verbal skills.

Jane Healy, Ph.D.
Endangered Minds

The central theme of Healy's book is that environment and culture, the model imperative again, affect both brain development and function. Supporting this is the pioneering research of Marion Diamond, professor of neuroanatomy at the University of California, Berkeley. Diamond says: "To those of us in the field, there is absolutely no doubt that culture changes brains, and there's no doubt in my mind that children's brains are changing."

Healy describes how new "advanced" standardized tests for today's ninth graders are significantly easier than what fourth graders were expected to read in 1964. The vast majority of young people are literate; few, however, can understand text above elementary school levels. Most are challenged when asked to draw inferences from basic texts, follow a sequence of ideas or articulate one's own argument based on a sequence of facts presented. The National Assessment of Educational Progress estimates that only 5 percent of high school graduates can satisfactorily master traditional college-level materials. Society and the job market are growing increasingly abstract and complex while the capacity to deal with complexity and abstraction is diminishing. What is the cause and what can we do?

Despite incontrovertible evidence that children who read well come from homes where reading is a prominent part of life; most parents do not read themselves. Eighty percent of the books in this country are read by about 10 percent of the people.

The proportion of readers in the United States is continuing to become smaller with a steady and significant decline in the number of book readers under twenty-one, according to Dr. Bernice Cullinan of New York University. She reports on one large group of "typical" fifth graders queried about the average time spent reading outside of school: 50 percent read for four minutes a day of less, 30 percent for two minutes per day or less, 10 percent read nothing. This same group of children watched an average of 130 minutes of television per day.

Each and every form of play is an exercise in metaphoric–symbolic thinking, the foundation of all literacy and higher learning.
Evolution's End

141

Yet, as Cullinan reminds us, children become good, insightful, analytic readers *only* by lots of practice with reading.

Our society is becoming increasingly aliterate, says Cullinan. An aliterate person is one who knows how to read but who doesn't choose to read. These are the people who glance at the headlines of a newspaper and grab the TV schedule. They do not read books for pleasure, nor do they read extensively for information.

We cite this example because it draws attention to three critical issues: 1. the relationship adult models have with written language, 2. the profound shift from the use of descriptive words to graphic images to communicate, which we see most dramatically in the shift from family conversation, storytelling, and the golden days of radio to television and computers, and 3. how these two influences, the model and the environment, conspire to affect brain development and behavior.

Jane Healy, Ph.D.
Endangered Minds

The average child in the United States sees six thousand hours of television by their fifth year, at which point, in the midst of what should be the high point of their dreamlike world of play, we put them in school, prevent bodily movement (most purposive learning is sensory-motor at this age), and demand they handle highly abstract-symbolic systems (alphabets and numbers) for which most of them have no neural structures at all. Driven by nature to follow their models, they try and can't. Their self-esteem collapses and failure and guilt give rise to anger. Even after beginning school their time-percentage of television viewing remains unabated. They spend more hours looking at television than attending school, and our national daily viewing time grows year by year.
Evolution's End

Descriptive words, symbols, and metaphors act as nutrients. They challenge and feed the developing brain, growing and expanding the capacity for imagination. Television and computer images, being concrete rather than abstract forms, are like junk food in this respect, empty calories that displace the nutrients needed for growth. The particular centers of the brain necessary for critical and creative thinking are not engaged while a person is viewing television and computer screens. A diet lacking abstract symbols and metaphors results in retarded growth of these brain centers. As with all development, the later stages are built upon and embedded in the formative stages.

The development of each brain center adds to the play of consciousness we call reality. Development, and therefore "reality," for a child born deaf or blind will be quite different from that of a child who can hear or see. As each new capacity unfolds and develops, it affects the nature and quality of those which came before and all that will follow. Opportunities, possibilities, and one's worldview for a literate person is profoundly different that for one who cannot read or write. The same is true for imagination. Content is not the issue. We are focusing on capacity and how the development of one capacity folds back and affects all other capacities, lifelong. The presence and development of imagination, or lack of those, profoundly affects everything that follows, and descriptive language is the key.

Language development begins before birth. The critical period for the development of imagination is early, approximately age two to seven or eight. Most of the "childlike" qualities Ashley Montagu describes in *Growing Young* involve imagination; curiosity, playfulness; willingness to experiment; flexibility; humor; receptiveness to new ideas; eagerness to learn. None of these qualities are reflexive. None emanate solely from the sensory motor or emotional brain centers. The later, more abstract brain centers interpret the flow of sensory and emotional data provided by the earlier brain systems and assign names or word/symbols for the more important experiences or states. We then participate in the creative process by using these words/symbols to stimulate mental images. The creative play of these images results in the discovery of new patterns and possibilities that we then use to change our environment. The inner affects the outer, which affects the inner in an unending reciprocal, creative dynamic. Fail to develop imagination and this expansive creative cycle ends. We literally can't imagine new forms and possibilities. We are stuck in a reflexive, mechanical, cause-and-effect world over which we have little control. Hope, the passionate vision of a new alternative, a better future, has no meaning whatsoever without imagination.

Of the range of capacities within a given species some individuals develop one set of capacities to a high degree, while others may develop very different abilities or skills. Elite athletes, for example, may run long distances with ease but be unable to balance their checkbooks. Poets may weave elaborate tapestries with words, but not be able to shoot a single hoop. As each capacity is developed, the internal image projected in consciousness by the senses and brain systems articulating that capacity change. We might say that the colors and intensity emanating from that capacity grow brighter, more acute and therefore play a more dominant role in perception. The range and variety of capacities are species-specific. The particular set of capacities each individual recognizes and develops is experience-dependent. It is in harmony with the model-environment.

Change the model, change the environment and the specific set of capacities developed changes with it, along with the internal image and one's worldview, which shapes all of one's relationships. And this reciprocal dynamic is going on every day, moment by moment, loping back, affecting our personal development as we affect the outer environment. Creator and created are locked in this mirroring, interdependent relationship.

In my book <u>Magical Child</u>, I discussed some of the critical problems facing technological countries today. These conditions are apparently brought about by imbalances of thought connected with technology itself. The problems I addressed have worsened sharply in the years since I completed it, until any hope of solution seems remote in our time. I need only mention the continued epidemic increase of infantile autism; childhood schizophrenia; brain damage and its mental-physical dysfunctions; the collapse of the family unit; the increase of suicides in children; the breakdown in classroom discipline and inability of young people to learn; these coupled with a general increase in social collapse and adult confusion.
Bond of Power

For millions of years this environment-development, creator-created relationship unfolded, manifesting as greater and greater capacity for abstraction. Human beings evolved, discovered fire, invented tools, created symbols, words and languages to stand in the place of things real and imagined. Very quickly these abstract symbols began to compete with the external environment as the source of internal imagery. Stories were created to flood the developing brain/mind with internal images not present to the sensory system. Schools were formed to nurture and cultivate and develop this capacity to imagine. In the mid-twentieth century this evolutionary drive stumbled.

Some ten years after we began to systematically separate infants from mothers in hospitals, eliminating bonding and breaking down development of the limbic-heart dynamic, we introduced television. The major damage of television [and by implication computers] has little to do with content. Its damage is neurological, and it has, indeed, damaged us, perhaps beyond repair.

Television replaced storytelling in most homes and transformed the radio from storyteller to a music box. Television also replaced family conversation in general. With television on the scene, parents rarely played with children. All sat around the box, and even playing among siblings disappeared. Thus no capacity for play and its internal imaging developed. Nintendo cannot replace imaginative play.

Television floods the brain with a counterfeit of the response the brain is supposed to learn to make to the stimuli of words or music. As a result, much of the structural coupling between mind and environment is eliminated; few metaphoric images develop; few higher cortical areas of the brain are called into play; few, if any, symbolic structures develop. $E=MC^2$ will be just marks on paper, for there will be no metaphoric ability to transfer those symbols to the neocortex for conceptualization, and subsequently, no development of its main purpose, symbolic conceptual systems.

Failing to develop imagery means having no imagination. This is far more serious than not being able to daydream. It means children who cannot "see" the inner image—what the mathematical symbol or the semantic words mean; nor the chemical formulae; nor the concept of civilization as we know it. They can't comprehend the subtleties of our Constitution or Bill of Rights and are seriously (and rightly) bored by abstractions of this sort. They can sense only what is immediately

Once a culture or person collapses into anxiety, no self-effort is effective against that negative power. Only insight has the power to override that negativity and bring the system into balance. Operation bootstrap always fails. Wholeness of mind can't come from any action or thought from a split person, but only through a kind of grace, the power of insight arriving full-blown into the brain.
Bond of Power

bombarding their physical system and are restless and ill at ease without such bombardment. Being sensory-deprived they initiate stimulus through constant movement or intense verbal interaction with each other, which is often mistaken for precocity but is actually a verbal hyperactivity filling the gaps of the habituated bombardments. [Which is to say, failure to develop imagination is a key factor in understanding our epidemic of attention-deficit disorders in young children.]

The average child in the United States sees six thousand hours of television by his or her fifth year, at which point, in the midst of what should be the zenith of their dream-like world of play, we put them in school, prevent bodily movement (most purposeful learning is sensory-motor at this age), and demand they handle highly abstract-symbolic systems (alphabets and numbers) for which most of them have no neural structures at all. Driven by nature to follow their models, they try and cannot. Their self-esteem collapses, and failure and guilt give rise to anger. Even after beginning school children's television time continues unabated. They spend more hours viewing television than attending school, and our national daily viewing time grows year by year.

By 1963 studies had shown a direct one-to-one correspondence between the content of television and behavior. Violence on television (and by implication on computers) produces violent behavior in young people. Everyone knows that. Once one has habituated to violence as a way of life, however, anything less is boring. There are sixteen acts of violence per hour of children's programming, only eight per hour on adults'. By the time our children become teenagers, they have seen an estimated 18,000 violent murders on television, their primary criteria for what is "real". Life is shown to be expendable and cheap, yet we condemn them for acting violently.

Evolution's End

Our criticism of television and computers, especially for the early child, has to do with the way these technologies create counterfeit images for processes the developing brain is designed to create itself. The basic rule of development holds: no challenge from the model environment, no development of that capacity.

The essence of imagination is play and it is this "free-play" of the mind and body that make imagination so important. Many adults unfortunately are themselves play-deprived. They lack imagination and an open-ended

The early child goes through a period of passionate intensity for naming everything he sees (the Whazzat Mamma? period). This is verbal-modeling, and the word given is the key that unlocks that particular part of the "barren chaos of nature" and grows an orderly arrangement with that brain, that is, forms a concept. The capacity of the word to lift things from the undifferentiated event into perceptional order is precisely what the child's brain needs to organize its world-view, and given, intern, a world for the child to view. In this way the movement from concreteness to abstraction is begun. The created order of thought will eventually be the eternal world of the human mind, the final matrix into which we must move when physical life is over. Bond of Power

145

playful response to life. There is the "right way" to do just about everything, and if life doesn't conform to the expected standard, well, you know what happens next: conflict, frustration and anger. Research found the same to be true of children. Children who developed imagination and play were less aggressive and violent than those who did not. Stuart Brown's research with convicted felons showed a similar correlation between the absence of imagination and play and aggression.

Retaining our childlike capacities as we mature—curiosity, playfulness; willingness to experiment; flexibility; humor; receptiveness to new ideas and a lifelong eagerness to learn—all involve imagination. Each time we respond to a child or to the world with these qualities, we are developing these qualities. Turning off the television is a great way to begin developing imagination. For many this represents a major challenge, which drives home the point of how addicted we have become to counterfeit imagery. Reading aloud age-appropriate literature with children helps. Talking to children during meals, describing one's own childhood experiences, inventing stories, planning-imagining a vacation, any use of descriptive language to create images, shared meaning and undreamed-of possibilities expand the field of imagination and all that it holds.

Recall how the emotional state of the mother determined the actual character, nature, and shape of her uterine infant's brain. Allan Schore shows how the same positive-negative directive determines the further growth, shape, and nature of the infant/toddler's brain in the first two years after birth as well. One of the major brain growth-spurts takes place after birth, and the fate of that new neural material is subject to the same model imperative as was that before birth. Use it or lose it, and the way the brain is used is the way it forms and grows.
The Biology of Transcendence

Principle Seven
Renewing
(Reincarnate Now)

This moment has never been before. Do we meet it with the same old pattern or with the wonder, excitement, and growth we felt as a child? Each of our principles: being attentive to being (the model imperative), safe enough to play (protecting, belonging, the safe place), inviting the unexpected (suspending assumptions), taking our cues from the child (the art of listening and observing), responding deeply and completely (authentic feelings and needs), and imagining, create a "crack" in our habits of body and mind. With that crack we become, if only for a moment, less mechanical. As if stepping foot into some new, unknown territory, we recognize that energy is there. We are attentive, alert, curious. All our attention, and vast intelligence, is gathered, ready to meet, learn and be transformed by the moment, deeply and completely. And what strange creature do we find? A changing reflection of ourselves and of the entire species, the child or children we love, the future of humanity.

146

Like a mime dancing with his or her reflection, each move is embodied by the other and in that instant both are transformed, and the transformation changes the next moment, and the cycle is repeated, transformation after transformation, moment by moment, dancing. Learning is taking place with each new "crack" in our habits, with each new perception. That learning is embodied and expresses, reincarnates, now.

This renewing principle was beautifully described earlier by David Bohm in a conversation with Rupert Sheldrake and Renee Weber. Bohm was describing quantum theory and the relationship between energy [mind] and matter. he used the analogy of a ballet and the music being played to illistrate how "meaning" organizes matter. In this case the meaning was the music and the dancers were matter.

> Electrons in a super-conducting state [perhaps what we are calling the *Zone* or optimum learning relationship] for example, move in a regular, coordinated way so they don't scatter. In an ordinary state, they are like a disorganized crowd of people. Now if you compare this to a ballet, you could say that in the super-conducting state, the wave function is like the *score,* which acts as a kind of information, and the dance is the meaning of the score…
>
> The meaning of the whole score is such that it determines how many independent dances are going on and what they are. To make this ballet dance analogy better, let's say that the wave function score is not fixed, but is a score, which depends on the initial configuration of the particles. The dance would vary according to the configurations of the dancers.

David Bohm
Dialogues with Scientists & Sages, by Renee Weber

When asked what he meant by the "wave-score" not being fixed, Bohm described how most often the conductor is reading sheets of music and that the dancers are moving in predetermined patterns. We might compare this to our normal modes of parenting, with its rewards and punishments. In Bohm's renewing analogy the conductor is creating the music spontaneously by sensing and responding to the configuration of the dancers and their movements. The dancers inspire the conductor who embodies that inspiration and expresses it as a new musical score. This new music inspires the dancers to move in new ways, which transforms the conductor—creator and created mirror one another in an unending dance of creative develop-

There is a relationship between what we think is out there in the world and what we experience as being out there. There is a way in which the energy of thought and the energy of matter modify each other and interrelate. A kind of rough mirroring takes place between our mind and our reality.
Crack In the Cosmic Egg

In trying to correct our error, we have to take our eyes off our course of development and concentrate on the error. Then several things happen. For one thing, we are now off course, going in a direction counter to our development. Our error has become our direction, and our pseudocourse. The error is not developmental of itself and the direction of error only leads to itself. We have stopped growth in mid-wobble. At that point, thought becomes detached from consciousness and insight-intelligence, which are the straight-line course. Thought tries to become self-sufficient of necessity, which is to say, thought in error tries to correct itself, rather than align itself again with the course of development Bond of Power.

ment. This renewing, transforming cycle encompasses all of our principles into a creative, flowing process.

This principle lifts the experience and the adult-child relationship out of mechanical, predetermined patterns and opens the door to lifelong learning, curiosity, playfulness, willingness to experiment, flexibility, and humor. Paraphrasing and applying David Bohm's essential description of science to parenting, we find that:

> Parenting consists of thought and action, which arises in creative perception and is expressed through play. This play unfolds into provisional behavior, which moves outward into action and returns as fresh perception and new insight. This process leads to continuous adaptation by the adult and the child, which undergoes constant growth, transformation, and extension. Relating to and mentoring children, therefore, is not something rigid and fixed that accumulates indefinitely in a steady way, but is a continual process of change. When serious contradictions in the adult-child relationship are encountered, it is necessary to return to creative perception and free play, which transforms the relationship and leads to new insight. Parenting, coaching and educating apart from this renewing, creative cycle inevitably leads to conflict.

And it is this conflict, and the implicit resistance it implies, that prevents us from being in the *Zone*, that optimum learning relationship, all the days of our lives.

Playful Parenting—The Optimum Learning Relationship

Mentoring the future of humanity is a gift, a profound responsibility and a tremendous challenge. It demands our very best each moment. Nothing less will do. Accepting this challenge means that adults must learn and grow right along with their children—easily said but difficult to do.

Understanding that play is the essence of true learning takes the sting out of this responsibility. Right and wrong, winning and failure have no place in true play. How could we fail as parents, as educators, and coaches if we are being fully present with children, if we are listening and responding deeply and completely, if we are curious, expecting the unexpected, learning from the moment and creating a new response based on what we just discovered?

When we learned to ride a bicycle, hit a baseball, to dance the tango, compute the circumference of a circle, drive a car, make love, build a house and a thousand other new things, did we not do just that, we gather all our attention and energy to meet the challenge completely? The difference is that children are constantly changing and so are we. To respond appropriately we need a model that is as flexible we are. With such a model mastery is not a fixed point. It a never-ending journey, a process, a dance, moving.

Mastery is that mysterious process where that which is difficult or even impossible to do becomes easy and even pleasurable through practice. Mastery is learning and learning what we are designed to do, lifelong. Mastery is open-ended. It is a journey where every mile we go along the path, the destination becomes two miles further away. New possibilities keep opening and expanding every step along the way.

All of life is a learning environment, especially when we have children. What could be better for our selves, for our children and our society than to have the full development and realization of every individual be our basic aim? And to approach this possibility with our own children is one of the greatest challenges and opportunities of all. It is the person who can really learn and change every day that wins at the game of life. Whether or not they're winning a particular contest doesn't matter at all, that person is winning all the time.

Personal Interview
George Leonard
Educator, Author: <u>Education & Ecstasy</u>, <u>Mastery</u>,
<u>This Life We are Given</u>

David Bohm once remarked that if Einstein saw more than Newton it was because he stood on Newton's shoulders. What better way for you and I to see far and wide, to develop our highest potential, than to hold our children as high as possible so we can see and explore the new world that they are creating? And play is the optimum state for this relationship to unfold. What an amazing, miraculous gift.

In-joy… Michael & Joe

State-religions form as survival strategies for the soul, and are the pseudo-sacred hand maidens of culture. Culture, myth and religion are brought about through our projections of our transcendent nature and in turn are the cause of our projections. Each effect is the cause of itself and each brings the other into being. All three interlocking systems are sustained by the periodic violence they generate within us…

The nature or character of a myth or religion is incidental to the force of the culture which both embodies and gives rise to myths and religions. And abandoning one myth or religion to embrace another has no effect on culture, which produces myth and religion automatically. Science supposedly supplanted religion, but simply became a new religious form, and an even more powerful cultural support, and an equal source of restraint on our spirit.

The Biology of Transcendence

References

Touch the Future Interview Index

Complete interviews with the individuals quoted, can be reviewed at Touch the Future's web site: ttfuture.org

Interviews in order of appearance	TTFuture interview link
Michael Murphy	TTFuture.org/murphy
Johnny Miller	TTFuture.org/miller
Ashley Montagu	TTFuture.org/montagu
Keith Buzzell, MD	TTFuture.org/buzzell
Fred Shoemaker	TTFuture.org/shoemaker
Jean Leidloff	TTFuture.org/leidloff
Barbara Fendeisen, MFCC	TTFuture.org/fendeisen
David Bohm, Ph.D.	TTFuture.org/bohm
John Douillard	TTFuture.org/douillard
O. Fred Donaldson, Ph.D.	TTFuture.org/donaldson
Bruce Lipton, Ph.D.	TTFuture.org/lipton
James W. Prescott, Ph.D.	TTFuture.org/prescott
Chuck Hogan	TTFuture.org/hogan
Stuart Brown, MD	TTFuture.org/brown
Bowen White, MD	TTFuture.org/white
Peter Jacobsen	TTFuture.org/jacobsen
Tom Lehman	TTFuture.org/lehman
George Leonard	TTFuture.org/leonard
Nancy Lopez	TTFuture.org/lopez
Davis Love III	TTFuture.org/love
Mike Reid	TTFuture.org/reid
Randy Henry	TTFuture.org/henry
Tim Gallewy	TTFuture.org/gallewy

Some interviews are off-line, pending approval.

Joseph Chilton Pearce

Reaching Beyond Magical Child

This broadcast quality series of six one-hour programs is the most comprehensive summary of Pearce's contribution to the field of child and human development available anywhere. Each program stands on its own. Together they represent a stunning overview of child and human development.

The Awakening of Intelligence
Joe begins by describing the nature of intelligence, brain development, and the critical role adults play in each stage of a child's development.

Pregnancy, Birth & Bonding
Here, Joe describes the miracle of pregnancy, birth and bonding, the optimal conditions for birth, the negative impact of unnecessary intervention and ways of providing the safest, most intimate experience for mother, baby and family.

Imagination & Play
Play is the most important activity for the early child. Joe explores how authentic play creates the foundation for all higher learning. He describes language development, the importance of imagination, storytelling and the adverse impact of television and computers during the early years.

Learning & Education
Joe contrasts true learning with the conditioning and behaviour modification found in many educational environments. True education is drawing out, challenging and developing a child's innate capacities rather that pouring in cultural or economic norms. Understanding the nature of real learning changes dramatically how we view schooling.

Critical & Creative Thinking
In this program Joe reaches beyond the limitations most adults have accepted for themselves by exploring human potentials few of us develop. Referencing the developmental stages, he describes insight and intelligence, true creativity and the capacity to think and reason without conflict.

Beyond Adolescence
The brain grows well into our late twenties, bringing changes in perception and behavior. Joe shares the idealism and passion found in adolescence, the despair many teens feel when their models fail to meet these high expectations, and what new possibilities may emerge beyond adolescence, including research involving the intelligence of the heart.

Six one-hour programs
See: ttfuture.org/reaching

Joseph Chilton Pearce
Mother-Infant Bonding
and The Intelligence of the Heart

Physicists describe fields of energy, how they imply meaning, information and intelligence. New research suggests that the heart field determines the general environmental conditions under which the genetic system spells out its instructions for new life. This brief program redefines bonding in light of this new research.

Up to sixty-five percent of the cells of the heart are neurons just like those found in the brain. There is a direct unmediated neuro-connection, a direct pipeline, between the heart and the brain. The brain informs the heart of its general emotional state and the heart encourages the brain to make an intelligent response. Poets and sages have been saying this about the heart down through the ages. The emerging field of neurocardiology and research at the Institute of HeartMath place the intelligence of the heart in the field of biology, where it belongs.

Each phase of the heartbeat creates its own part of the field effect that surrounds the body. The first is very short, close to the heart. The next radiates outward at least three feet and is very powerful. The third field extends twelve to fifteen feet from the body. It is easy to see that one person's field will often overlap another's. When two fields overlap they interact. This resonant field effect is present in every relationship, but is particularly important for mothers and infants. The meaning of the fields shared by mother and infant contain a great deal of critical information for both.

That heart fields interact and entrain is a precise, measurable, scientific fact. The amplitude and the Hertz value of the two heart frequencies become coherent, creating a state of harmony, wholeness and health. When the infant's heart and the mother's heart are entrained, their brain structures also become synchronized. We refer to this balanced state as bonding between mother and infant. Failing the initial bond with the mother, all subsequent bonding is not only put at risk but is very difficult to bring about. Studies at Harvard show that the nature of our early bonds are reflected throughout life, both in one's health and ability to interact socially.

Allan Schore describes how the first eighteen months determine the subsequent moves of the intelligence. Why? Because the emotional experience the child is given during the first eighteen months determines the nature and quality of the neural structures that develop in that period. Emotional nurturing translates directly into the field effect, shared or not shared, with the immediate environment. During those first eighteen months that environment is mother, father, and other primary caregivers. This video compliments and expands upon *The Origins of Love & Violence*, Jim Prescott's pioneering research at NIH on early mother-infant separation, bonding and the developing brain.

8.5 minutes
See: ttfuture.org/heart

155

Discovering
The Intelligence of Play

The Intelligence of Play is a revolutionary model of optimum learning, performance and wellness for children and adults. Learn how to apply what athletes call *The Zone* to parenting and education. Discover why some perform at extraordinary levels while others, with equal talent, find life a constant struggle. The Intelligence of Play will revolutionize how you look at optimum learning and peak performance, in any field, at any age.

Joseph Chilton Pearce On Optimum Learning Relationships

We have conditioning, like Pavlov's conditioning of his dogs, and behavior modification, which we call learning but it's not learning. It's conditioning. Real learning takes place by what Maria Montessori called "the absorbent mind of the child." Children simply absorb their universe, absorb it and become it, and they do this through play.

O. Fred Donaldson, Ph.D. On Contest & Competition

Original play is a practice of kindness, which permeates all of one's relationships. It cultivates an ever-renewing sense of enchantment and engagement with the world. It develops calmness, awareness and a flexible ability to handle stress, surprise or challenges without aggression.

Stuart Brown, M.D. On Play, Natural Learning & Aggression

Play states, as they have appeared in nature, are the major driving force in the development of higher brain function and critical for normal and healthy socialization, flexibility and adaptability. The greater the skill of the player in nature, the larger and more intricate is their brain. Authentic play is essential for adaptive learning.

Chuck Hogan On Play as Peak Performance

Security is the foundation of play and the key to unlocking our unlimited potentials. We need to create ways for children to discover play for the joy of play, to enter into it freely and play the game so that the playing is winning. If adults can't have fun, children aren't going to have fun. If we've got to win to prove we're having fun, they'll have to win to have fun. The question is not so much what kids need to do, it is what we need to do.

James W. Prescott, Ph.D. On Nurturing & Brain Development

Physical affection and intimacy begin with mother and father and are the foundations for basic trust or its absence, fear and aggression. Safety, close physical contact, affection and bonding play critical roles in early brain development. These early relationships create life-long patterns of expansive learning or self-defense and violence. Basic trust is a prerequisite for The Intelligence of Play.

90 minutes
See: ttfuture.org/play

Golf & The Intelligence of Play

Hosted by Peter Jacobsen

Athletics & the Intelligence of Play represents a powerful tool to reach 20 million parents, coaches and young players. Featuring the personal experiences of world class athletes, visionary coaches and educators, *Golf & The Intelligence of Play* helps adults and children develop optimal learning relationships in any field, at any age. The program brings out the very best in any player and returns *love of the game* back to athletics. This 60 minute broadcast quality program is a must for any parent, coach or young player involved in amateur athletic programs.

> *Play can be the most serious undertaking of a child's life because they're laying down the foundation for the later forms of intelligence.*

Joseph Chilton Pearce
Author of *The Magical Child*

The real secret is the love of the game. If you love it, you'll always beat the person that wants it for power and glory and money.

Johnny Miller
PGA Hall of Fame

> *I learned to find peace on the golf course at an early age. I think that's why I've done so well.*

Nancy Lopez
LPGA Hall of Fame

Just look at the little league games, parents in the middle of the playing field screaming at the kids, "Why didn't you win?" It's a disaster.

Chuck Hogan
Educator, Coach, Author

> *Much of what we do with children ends up reinforcing their feelings of inadequacy. The very thing we don't want to do we end up dong simply because we're doing with them what was done with us.*

Bowen White, M.D.
Author, Educator, Clown

My dad was great at teaching me to learn from my mistakes. He was always focusing on the positive. "You played 16 holes as good as anybody can play golf. Now, here's what we need to work on.

Davis Love III
PGA Champion

60 minutes
See: ttfuture.org/golf

James W. Prescott, Ph.D.

The Origins of Love & Violence

Direct contact, ideally with mother, her touch, movement, voice, body and facial expressions, her taste and smell, act as nutrients that shape a baby's physical, emotional, sexual and cognitive brain systems. Learn why brain research challenges many assumptions regarding bonding and early childcare policies.

Part I – Physical Pleasure, Bonding & Basic Trust (13 minutes.)

Part I summarizes Prescott's fifteen-years of pioneering research at NIH on the biological roots of violence, mother-infant separation and the developing brain. Jim describes how early bonding, nurturing touch, movement and breast feeding encode the developing brain for a lifetime of affectionate relationships. Rare and dramatic images, from the award-winning documentary *Rock-A-By Baby,* link permanent abnormalities in the brain to mother-infant separation, abuse and early neglect. This research summary and Pearce's *Intelligence of the Heart* redefines "bonding" as a biological imperative.

Part II – Collection of Four Historical Programs (48 minutes)

Part II includes the original 30 minute version of **Rock-A-By Baby** premiered first at the 1970 White House Conference on Children. This rare documentary highlights the emotional-psychological devastation of the failure of physical affectional bonding in the maternal-infant relationship in animals and humans. Brain-behavioral abnormalities are vividly dramatized in rhesus monkeys as a consequence of mother-infant separation.

Child Abuse, CTV Toronto (11 minutes) provides an overview of the Somatosensory Affectional Deprivation theory of peace and violence. Explicit medical photos of abused children; a five second clip of the rape scene from "Clock Work Orange" and some natural nudity in primitive tribal cultures are shown. The video provides dramatic documentation that brain cell abnormalities were present in these mother deprived monkeys. This rare film footage is not available anywhere else.

Happy Babies, (7 minutes) interview with Connie Chung, Dr. Prescott and Suzanne Arms describes specific parenting practices to assure maternal-infant bonding. The television news broadcast features mothers describing how breastfeeding provides unusual emotional bonding with their infants.

Neuropsychology of Affectional Bonding (5 minutes) interview discussing the neuropsychology of sensory stimulation and deprivation upon brain- behavioral development and why touching, hugging and carrying one's infant/child on the body of the mother, father or caretaker (vestibular-cerebellar stimulation) are essential for normal brain development and function and, thus, normal emotional-social development of the infant/child.

13 minutes and 48 minutes
See: ttfuture.org/origins

David B. Chamberlain, Ph.D. & Suzanne Arms
Babies Know More Than You Think

Ours is the first generation to have scientific information about life before birth. Babies learn and remember more and much earlier than we ever-imagined. Understanding this research can profoundly impact pregnancy, birth, bonding and beyond. This **60 minute video** describes how the attitudes, beliefs and emotional states of mom and dad affect the unborn baby and what can be done to insure optimum growth during this first frontier of development.

We would have a very different world if mothers and fathers understood what a miraculous time this is for themselves and for their infants. This program gives birth back to women and their rightful place in society.
Joseph Chilton Pearce
Author: *The Magical Child*

This conversation needs to occur in every home, school and community center. Thank you for presenting these truths with courage.
Jeanine Parvati Baker
Midwife, Author: *Conscious Conception*

Love the program. I found the content informative, interesting and enthralling. So much beneficial information for new parents. It's delightful to watch.
Pamela Shrock, Ph.D, P.T.
Director, Psychosomatic OB/GYN, Winthrop University Hospital

A copy of this program should be sent to the department heads of all OB/GYN programs as well as to the directors of pediatric programs.
Herbert H. Nasdor, M.D.
Lutherville, Maryland

David Chamberlain, PhD.
is a psychologist and major contributor to the field of pre and perinatal psychology. He is the author of *The Mind Of Your New Born Baby* and over forty professional papers on the consciousness of the unborn child.

Suzanne Arms
helped pioneer a national social movement by bringing important information about the process of birth to women, men and health care providers. She is the author of 7 books, a photojournalist and tireless advocate for midwifery and home and community-based birth. Her book, *Immaculate Deception,* sold more that 200,000 copies and was named "Best Book of the Year" by the New York Times.

60 minutes
See: ttfuture.org/babies

to erode the fixed boundaries and prejudgments implicit in our adult agendas. The principles are not, therefore, formulas, fixed rules, or even guidelines. We are not telling you "how to" raise your children. On the contrary, we are assuming competence and affirming that you and your child possess and embody infinite intelligence. Our principles, like Zen koans or other mystery school techniques, help dissolve the resistance, the unnecessary boundaries, and the limitations imposed by our beliefs, our prejudgments. Eliminating resistance restores the mind, body, and emotions to their natural order. Perhaps this shift of state can be compared to the reset button on your computer. When the data of various programs, which can be compared to our beliefs, create conflicts, the operating system of the computer locks up or becomes less efficient. Pressing the reset button clears out the conflicting data and restores the system to its original, optimum performance. The shift of awareness from conflict to play resets the entire organism and redefines its relationship to the universe. And from this original mind or state we meet the child, this moment, as he is, not only as we "think" he should be.

Studies show that a teacher's underlying belief about seven-year-old students has a profound impact on them. Children will do well under a teacher who believes in them and "knows" they will do well, and poorly under a negative teacher whose opinion of the child (and probably self) is low. Just as our own attitudes, of which we need not be aware, can impact our health and relationships, they can impact our children.
Evolution's End

Principle One
Being Attentive to Being
(The Model Imperative)

Being Attentive to Being expands awareness to hold and value our agenda and our state of being simultaneously. Adults often focus exclusively on their agenda, ignoring the actual state of their relationship. *Being Attentive to Being* includes both agenda and state. Bringing greater attention to the moment demands greater awareness and sensitivity. Being more present is a profound change in state, one that is less reflexive, less mechanical. Capacity expands with greater attention. Our lives and our relationships become multidimensional.

Being Attentive to Being recognizes and incorporates the model imperative, stage- and state-specific learning, multiple realities and intelligences, nonmaterial fields of influence and meaning in the relationship. It encourages adults to *be* the change they wish to see in others rather than demanding that others conform to their expectations. Applying this principle is helpful at any age, but is particularly important when relating to younger children. The more concrete their experience, the more important this principle

Index

accepted, unconditionally, 101
act, to, 139
ADHD, 79-80
adult agenda, 7,120-121, 127, 129, 137
Albert, David, Ph.D., 120
And The Skylark Sings With Me, D. Albert, 120
anxiety, 33, 49
approval of others, 82
associative function of the brain, 133
assumptions, 30, 133-134
athletics & the intelligence of play, 90
attention, 32
attention deficit disorders, 145
awakening of intelligence, 137
awareness, 32
Bannister, Roger, 42, 104, 105
Barbara Findeisen, 29
basic trust, 50
be attentive to being, 129
Be Here Now, Ram Dass, 138
becoming, 137
Beethoven, 72
beginner's mind, 39
beliefs, 29
belonging, 131
Bettleheim, Bruno, 58
Bible, the, 133
Bill of Rights, the, 144
Billy Jean King, 42
Blake, William, 72
Body, Mind & Sport, J. Douillard, 42
Bohm, David, Ph.D., 10, 29, 34, 37, 39, 45, 74, 108, 124, 136, 140, 147-149
bonding, 25, 120
bonding, maintaining, 21
bonding, adult-child, 54
bonding, as learning, 53
bonding, during pregnancy, 25
bonding, mother, 25

boundaries, 8, 25, 104, 123
brain, 14-15, 17
brainwave activity, 117
Briggs, John, Ph.D., 9, 10
Brown, Stuart, M.D., 67, 85-86
Buzzell, Keith, M.D., 16
chaos, theory, 7-9
Chaplin, Charlie, 72
child of the dream, 64
childlike qualities, 12-13, 127, 143
coach, the, 69, 103
comparison, 43
competition, 43, 98
computers, 140, 145
conflict, 118, 128
Constitution, the, 144
contest culture, 80
Continuum Concept, J. Leidloff, 22
creativity, 10
Csikszentmihaly, Mihaly, Ph.D., 44, 77-78
culture, transforming, 106
curiosity, 7
Damasio, Antonio, M.D., Ph.D., 16-18
Dass, Ram (Richard Alpert, Ph.D.), 138
Death Star, 40
development, spiritual, 8
developmental stages, 24
devolution, 26
Dialogues with Scientists and Sages, R. Webber, 34
Diamond, Marian, Ph.D., 22, 141
discipline, 6
do it yourself, 69
Doing Nothing, Steven Harrison, 138
"don't try, do", 33
Donaldson, O. Fred, Ph.D., 45, 53, 59, 60, 67, 81-82, 84, 91, 99, 138-139
Douillard, John, 42, 92, 104
Eastern philosophy, 129
Education & Ecstasy, G. Leonard, 149

161

Einstein, 140, 149
Emotional Intelligence, D. Goleman, 128
empathy, increased, 108
Endangered Minds, J. Healy, 140
energy [mind] and matter, 147
Enriching Heredity, M. Diamond, 22
entertainment, 69
entrainment, 37
environmental signals, 26
Esalen Institute, 4, 39
eternal present, 138
ETM (Education Through Music), 63, 64, 65, 72
evolution, 25, 123
experience, love of the, 102
Extraordinary Golf, 131
feeling safe, 20
field effect, 34, 37
fields of meaning, 34
fields, sharing, 35
flashes of insight, 40
Flow, the Psychology of Optimal Experience,
  M. Csikszentmihaly, 3, 40, 44-45, 77
Force, the, 40
Future Shock, A. Toffler, 137
Gallwey, Tim, 104
Gardner, Howard, 128
Goleman, Daniel, 128
groupies, 68
Growing Young, A. Montagu, 143
Harlow, Harry, 56
Harrison, Steven, 138
Healy, Jane, Ph.D., 140-142
heart, mother-infant bonding, 38
heart, the intelligence of, 36
Henry, Randy, 104
Hogan, Ben, 59
Hogan, Chuck, 59, 73, 95, 102, 103, 105
humanity, future of, 146
identity, 18
identity, individual, 20

162

imagery, counterfeit, 145
images, 17
images, internal, 15
images, as resonant representation, 15
images, counterfeit, 71, 145
imagination, 13, 140
imagine, 14
In the Zone, Transcendent Experience in Sports
  M. Murphy, R. White, 46
insight, 9, 116
insight-intelligence, 39
Institute of HeartMath, 37
intelligence, 14, 30, 134
intelligences, multiple, 128
invite the unexpected, 133
"it's all about control", 79
Jacobsen, Peter, 86
Japanese, Taiko, 26
Jerome, John, 105
Jordan, Michael, 42
Kennell, John, 53
Kitty Hawk, 106
Klaus, Marshall, 53
Kohn, Alfie, 76-78
Krishnamurti, J, 47-48, 137-138, 140
Lacey, John and Beatrice, 36
leader, following the, 95
learning, holistic, 128
learning, primary, 76
learning, stage specific, 24
Lehman, Tom, PGA, 92
Leidloff, Jean, 22-23, 50-52
Leonard, George, 99, 149
Lipton, Bruce, Ph.D., 48-49, 117, 132
listening, the art of, 135
Little League, 27, 83, 96
Lopez, Nancy, 100
Lord's Prayer, the, 133
love, 11
love and violence, origins of, 55

Love III, Davis, 101
MacLean, Paul, 15, 60
Magical Chid, J. Pearce, 24
magical children, 3
magical parents, 3
magical parents – magical athletes, 99
mastery, 149
Mastery, G. Leonard, 149
McLuhan, Marshall, 71, 130
Mead, Margaret, 72
memory, 17, 29, 30
metaphoric thinking, 63
Miller, Alice, 119
Miller, Johnny, 5, 100
mind, industrial, 106
model environment, 25
model imperative, 24, 57, 115, 129
monkey see – monkey do, 63
Montagu, Ashley, Ph.D., 11, 13, 20, 22, 30, 85, 126-127, 143
Montessori, Maria, 43, 49, 114
motivation, extrinsic (outside), 93
motivation, intrinsic (inside), 93
multi-dimensional human beings, 128
Murphy, Michael, 4-5, 43, 90
National Geographic, 85
National Institutes of Health, 36
nervous system, human, 15
neurocardiology, 37
Newton, 149
no grown-ups allowed, 68
not know, to, 136
Obi-Wan Kenobe, 40
observing, the art of, 135
optimum learning and performance, 43
Optimum Learning Relationships, 3-15, 19, 46, 49, 75, 76, 97, 104, 107-108, 120, 131, 135
optimum state, 4
Orr, David W., Ph.D., 106-107
oxytocin, 56
parenting, as battle, 134

parenting, in the zone, 27
Parents and Teachers Against Violence in Education, 88
patterns, predetermined, 126-127, 134
Peat, David F., Ph.D., 9, 10, 29, 45, 74
Piaget, 114
play, 3, 45, 58, 131
   ages & stages, 60
   as learning , 101
   deprivation & violence, 85
   abstract, 74
   adult, 73
   as learning, 42
   authentic defined, 44
   computer, 70
   creative, 74
   high chair, 61
   original, 41, 83
   practice & work, 59
   rough & tumble, 66
   sacred, 75
   safe enough to, 131
   smiles, 61
   television, 70
   the art of, 72
   the intelligence of, 43
   transcendent, 75
   talk, 64
Playing by Heart, O.F. Donaldson, 45
pre-judge, to, 127
Prescott, James W., Ph.D., 54-55, 57
Primacy, of states, 32
primary learning, 28, 57-58
Project NoSpank, 88
proprioception, 18
protecting, 131
provisional, 125
Punished by Rewards, A. Kohen, 76
punishment, 11, 75
punishment, corporal, 86
quantum fields, 34

quantum theory, 148
reflex system, 30, 136
reflexes, 29
Reid, Mike, 101
"reincarnate now", 137, 146
renewing (reincarnate now), 146
resonant field effect, 38
responding deeply & completely, 137
rewards, 11, 75
Riak, Jordan, 88
safe place, feeling, 69, 101, 131
Schore, Allan, Ph.D., 21, 30, 60
Science, Order & Creativity, D. Bohm & D. Peat, 10, 45
score, focusing on the, 86
self, as self-defense, 20
self, autobiographical, 19
self, image, 18-20, 22, 31, 94-95, 136,
self, origins of, 21
self, psychological, 19
self, social, 21
self-esteem, 108
Seven Life Lessons of Chaos, J. Briggs & D. Peat, 9
shame, 21, 146
Sheldrake, Rupert, Ph.D., 147
Shoemaker, Fred, 131-132
Skywalker, Luke, 40
startle effect, 133
state of being, 6, 27,
state specific learning/performance, 27, 34
states, as content, 33
states, local and non-local, 35
states, optimum, 130
Steiner, Rudolph, 65, 74
storytelling, 63
taking cues from the child, 9, 135-136
Tarahamara Indians, 42
television, 140, 144-146
television, behavior, 145
television, violence on, 145
The Power of Now, T. Eckhart, 138

The Unfettered Mind, Takuan Soho, 40-41
This Life We are Given, M. Murphy, G. Leonard, 149
thought, self-generative, 39
three's a crowd, 65
toddlers, 62
Tolle, Eckhart, 138
Tollfer, Alvin, 137
Touch the Future, 121
transcendence, 26
transformation, 11
transforming ourselves, 106
violence, reduced, 108
Waldorf education, 72
Weber, Rene, 34, 147
what will they think of me, 83
White, Bowen, M.D., 83, 92, 98
White, Burton, 64
White, Rhea A., 4, 46
Whitman, Charles, 85
winning and losing , 98
wonder, 7
wonder, watching with, 102
Woods, Tiger, 90
Wright Brothers, 106
yogic philosophy, 39
Zen philosophy, 39, 129
Zone, the, 3-4, 44-45, 58, 82, 131